Intellectu

Revolution

Intellectual Property Revolution

Successfully manage your IP assets, protect your brand and add value to your business in the digital economy

SHIREEN SMITH

R3THINK PRESS

First published in the United Kingdom in 2015 by Rethink Press

Praise

"This book offers a comprehensive, accessible myth-busting guide to IP that every entrepreneur should read. Could ultimately save a fortune."

———Paul Grant

Entrepreneur, Founder of The Funding Game

"If you want to scale your business, you need to know how to exploit your IP – the digital economy has changed the rules and Shireen makes it easy to understand how you can play to win."

———Jacqueline Biggs

Co-founder of Brand-camp.com and International Best Selling Author of *Marketing to Win*

"This is an easy to read book that really helped me understand how Intellectual Property is the crucial foundation of any successful business. It's a must read for any ambitious business or entrepreneur."

———Leigh Ashton

Author of *iSell* and Co-Founder of Sasudi.com

"This book was a bit of an eye-opener for me and gave me a whole new perspective on how IP can help build value into a business. It is now on my clients 'Must Read' list."

——Richard White

Founder, Business Development Academy

"I had not fully appreciated the importance of the IP in my business, or how it could help me to position myself correctly and succeed in a much bigger way. Shireen's book makes it clear that IP is the foundation of most modern business, and is full of straightforward information and practical advice - a must read for any business owner looking to grow and scale their business."

——Marianne Page

Creator of Bright 7 and Author of *Process to Profit*

Contents

Introduction

For years it baffled me why agencies creating Intellectual Property (IP) for businesses through branding and website development didn't universally appreciate the central relevance of intellectual property during the creative process.

Often, agencies I came across would advise their clients to consult their own lawyer on the name chosen, or once the work was concluded they would suggest their clients consult a lawyer to protect their brand. However, by then it's too late for an IP lawyer to add any real value beyond registering the IP. And the vast majority of businesses don't in fact go on to consult a lawyer anyway, either not bothering to register their rights, or doing the work themselves.

So, my last book, *Legally Branded,* aimed to provide accessible information about IP so more branding agencies, and business owners would know to take IP into account from an early stage. In hindsight, I think the level of detail in that book made it more of a reference book than one you might read cover to cover. So, I wanted to write an easier to read book.

At the same time, after the book had been published, I became aware that many entrepreneur groups, and business advisers were also failing to take IP into account. It was sometimes such a glaring omission that I couldn't understand why they didn't appreciate the relevance of IP issues to what they were teaching their business clients.

It then dawned on me that the problem was far bigger than I'd initially realised when I wrote *Legally Branded*. It went far beyond the branding industry.

So I decided to write another book. This was initially going to be called 'Intellectual Property – The Elephant in the Room'. However, as I researched the book I began to realise that something far more fundamental than lack of awareness of IP was at play.

For example, I came across a piece by Neil J Wilkof, an experienced IP lawyer who contributes to blogs such as IPKAT and IP Finance. Neil was discussing the absence of IP in MBA courses, and had this to say on the issue:

'It remains my most vexing professional challenge. The "it" is how to integrate IP/IC into management education. The vexation comes from the seeming paradox that while intellectual property and intellectual capital are routinely described as cornerstones of innovation, if not modern business itself, their systematic presence in MBA curricula remains sporadic at best.'

Neil's comment mirrored my own surprise about the neglect of IP law in entrepreneur groups.

On the one hand, the importance of intellectual property was emphasised, and yet I frequently heard experienced business advisers making comments like 'if you don't have £50,000 plus to spend on patents, forget it' (as if patents are the sum total of IP), or that 'IP is of course very important for businesses in the creative industries', or that 'IP is relevant once a business has a turnover of £300,000 plus'.

Then it struck me why society wasn't taking on board the importance of IP. It simply hasn't caught up quickly enough with the dramatically changed role of IP law in the digital age. The internet or web as I prefer to call it (although web referred to the browser initially, nowadays the term is synonymous with 'internet'), is creating new rules for many industries, as well as for the subject of IP law.

As I'll explain in this book, the digital revolution has made IP law relevant in ways that it wasn't in the industrial age. Despite the UK Government commissioning the Hargreaves Review of Intellectual Property and Growth in 2010 to ensure the UK has an IP framework best suited to supporting innovation and promoting economic growth in the digital age, there is still a marked lack of awareness in the business community about intellectual property, and what it means.

Indeed when people hear the phrase 'intellectual property', the term either means nothing to them, or it conjures up their preconceptions of what IP law is all about. Unless you're an IP lawyer focused on digital issues, you are unlikely to connect up why IP is relevant to every business in our digital world.

In an industrial society IP may have been an esoteric subject; one that was far from central to every business large or small. However, the growth of the knowledge economy means that IP is an asset class relevant to everyone. For example, the risk of encroaching on other people's rights is far greater nowadays. So, it's time to update our definitions, and in this book I'll sometimes refer to

IP as 'digital IP' as a way of separating it from the IP that people normally associate with the words – namely registration of patents, trade marks, and designs.

Much of the information contained in this book consists of my personal impressions as a solicitor practising law and running my own law firm in 2015; it is not meant to be scholarly or comprehensive.

My main aim in writing it is to highlight the importance of IP in the new economy so businesses take proper account of it. There would be a lot fewer business failures if they did, and the successful ones would enjoy more spectacular success if they involved a digital IP lawyer when implementing their ideas, and particularly when choosing a name.

The focus of the book is on general legal principles. IP law is an international subject as I discuss later in the book. So, people from countries outside the UK can benefit from the material in this book, even if some of the details of the laws or examples cited may be more appropriate to a UK audience.

Who this book is for

All Entrepreneurs and Small Business Owners need an insight into the relevance of digital IP, and this book is targeted at the following in particular:

■ Founders of new and existing businesses.

■ Senior executives.

■ Marketing directors.

■ Branding, design and web agencies who create IP for SMEs.

The information in this book will help you to understand digital IP issues sufficiently in order to be strategic about IP.

Chapter 2 discusses the changing legal industry due to the internet and deregulation, while chapter 3 looks at the different professionals engaged in IP work. Although these are relevant to buyers of legal services, if you are primarily interested in knowing why IP is of central relevance in the digital economy, you could skip those chapters, and just refer to them when needed.

Part One

Changing Role of IP and Lawyers in a Digital World

Chapter 1

IP Revolution in the Digital World

It was as I looked for answers to the question of why IP was so neglected in entrepreneurship circles and MBA courses that I realised that just as the digital revolution has changed the rules for many industries, so it has also changed the relevance of Intellectual Property (IP) – a subject that many still regard as quite esoteric.

During my research I found that out of twenty top start-up business books released between 2006 and 2013 only eight even mentioned IP, and of those, only a mere handful explored the subject beyond a cursory summary.

It was a similar story when I looked at MBA courses. The one run at London Business School is ranked number four in the world according to the Financial Times. Yet it does not mention IP in its core modules.

Why is IP being dealt with so inadequately despite its importance for every business, whether pre-start-up or mature?

In the UK alone there are more than half a million new companies registered every year. Yet many of these start-ups are completely unaware of what IP even means, some of which probably go under or achieve less success as a result.

The world has changed

Society hasn't caught up quickly enough with the dramatically changed role of IP law in the digital age.

A simple search on the web will instantly reveal whether a name or image you are using belongs to someone else. While in the industrial age you might have got away with infringing on other people's IP because nobody was likely to find out about you, now that everything is out in the open, it is no longer possible to ignore copyright and trade mark issues, even if you are a small start-up.

However, it is not just because you could be infringing on somebody else's rights that you need to take account of IP. In the overcrowded world of business, it is important to stand out with distinctive names, and to understand how to position yourself for commercial success.

You want to be able to scale your business through licensing or other commercialisation activities. These all depend on having secure IP rights, and understanding IP is essential to knowing how to protect your business against inevitable copying by competitors if you are successful.

So, avoiding infringing on others' rights, and using IP rights to protect your unique business proposition are crucially relevant to any ambitious business both before it starts out, and on an ongoing basis as the business progresses.

Many professions have yet to take it on board that the Internet is changing the rules. For example, the legal profession still treats IP law as a specialist topic, and therefore IP is not a core subject in the academic training of lawyers in the UK. This means that as a client approaching a lawyer, you can't assume they are all equally able to advise you.

In the new world we live in, it is as important to choose lawyers who have a solid grounding in IP, as it is to choose a conveyancing solicitor who has a solid understanding of physical property laws. With the latter you can take it as read that your solicitor will have studied land law, but when it comes to business and commercial lawyers, it isn't safe to assume your solicitor has the depth of expertise in IP law that you need in order to receive adequate IP advice. So, unless they have studied IP law and practised in that area you would be well advised to find specialist IP lawyers to do an audit of your business and advise you on the risks and opportunities.

When I was a law student in the late 70s, IP hardly featured in our studies. I remember reading a passage about it in one of our land law books, and that was the sum total the syllabus taught us about IP.

The subject of IP didn't really come to my consciousness again after I left university until I became an in-house lawyer at Reuters in the late 80s. As a news and media company, the everyday subjects we dealt with were general commercial, intellectual property and information technology law.

Several years later I studied IP at Masters' level, taking Information technology, ecommerce, copyright law, trade mark, and other IP courses. So, when I subsequently set up Azrights, it was inevitable that I would focus on IP law.

Having now run Azrights as an IP firm for ten years, I can confidently tell you that IP is central to every business. Yet educators of future lawyers still treat it as a specialist area.

Without IP training, tomorrow's lawyers will be no better equipped than general commercial lawyers are today, to advise businesses on copyright, names, websites and internet related legal issues. These are intrinsic to the needs of businesses nowadays. Advice on them should be available through every commercial lawyer. Only then would you as a client of a law firm receive the rounded advice you need on IP law. Failing that, general commercial lawyers who properly understand IP law would know to refer you to a specialist digital IP firm for an audit and further advice, even if they themselves have given you 'first aid' IP help.

The transition from industrial to digital economy has therefore impacted the skills lawyers need.

IP law will eventually become a compulsory subject taught to all law students, not just to those who are interested in taking it as an optional module. However, it will take time for those who make these decisions to effect the necessary changes. In the meantime, I recommend consulting what I call a 'digital IP' law firm. This is a term to distinguish the IP advice you might expect from a firm of patent and trade mark attorneys or a firm of general business lawyers, from the IP advice offered by an IP lawyer who understands the digital dimension of business.

We live in a world where reportedly more than 70% of corporate value is intangible. A world where some 70% of businesses are in the services sector, providing knowledge based products. If you are one of these businesses, chances are that your currency is information, ideas and know-how rather than physical assets. So, your success is impacted by the exploitation of your knowledge, as well as by such matters as who you know, and what opportunities you have to collaborate with others.

In terms of IP help, it's not enough to simply register rights. You also need appropriate agreements and advice so you are able to successfully commission the technology on which your business relies, and manage your relationships with outsourcers, clients, partners and more.

For physical products, the internet is an important distribution channel, so SMEs want lawyers who not only help them identify and protect their IP, but also understand the online space. If your business is online, then make sure your lawyer can advise on the impact of the web and social media upon it.

In the digital world there are few areas of commerce that are not impacted by IP as this book indicates. IP law is relevant in ways, in which it was not in the industrial age, so whenever you see a reference to digital IP in this book, understand that it is used to emphasise the difference from the traditional treatment of IP, which tends to focus on the registration of patents, trade marks, and designs.

At this point it might be relevant to briefly define what we mean by intellectual property.

What are Intellectual Property Rights?

I know from experience that many entrepreneurs and company executives do not know what intellectual property (IP) rights are, or if they do, they are often not so clear about them and would benefit from a reminder. So a definition of IP is worth including here.

IP is an umbrella term encompassing a range of legal rights that you can't see and touch (intangibles), notably:

■ **Trade marks** which protect names and other 'signs' used to identify products and services and distinguish them from those of competitors. An example of a sign is a word or logo. Names and slogans can be trade marks if they pass various requirements of the law. As they are not protected by copyright, branding agencies who develop new names will not have rights over the name itself. The name will function as the trade mark of the business that uses it, and will not be the property of the person who first thought of it. Names and signs must be distinctive to meet the legal criteria for trade mark protection, and may be registered within legally defined classes of goods and services. They are important ways of protecting brands – a term which is sometimes assumed to be relevant only to big business. In fact, every business has a brand whether it knows it or not.

■ **Copyright** protects a wide range of material, including websites, software, and content. Protection arises automatically, without the need for registration, as long as the work is 'fixed' in a permanent form (e.g. in writing). Copyright is the most universal of rights, covering written materials, music, art, logos, and computer programs, to name a few. Every business will have copyright and will use copyright belonging to others, so it is essential to get a broad understanding of how copyright works. There are surprising rules within copyright law which may mean that ownership will not be with the person you might assume.

■ **Patents** protect inventions for products or processes. To qualify for protection the invention must be new, have an inventive step not obvious to someone with experience and knowledge of that area, and be capable of industrial application. If an invention is protected with a patent, it means that nobody may make the product covered by the patented technology unless they obtain permission from the patent owner, or find a way round the patent to achieve the same end. So, with patents it is as important to be the first to file for protection, as it is to specify the innovation in ways that make it difficult for competitors to get round the patent. Patent law does not protect certain types of invention - for example, those relating to animal or plant varieties.

- **Designs** protect the visual appearance of a product or part of it. These rights do not protect the underlying concept of the product, however. To qualify for protection a design must be new and distinctive. Design registration protects the visual aspects of things like handbags or the shapes of packaging, or surface decoration of goods. Even logos may be registered. There are strict time limits within which to register designs. Doing so offers advantages over unregistered design rights.

- **Ancillary rights** is simply intended as a catch all term to refer to a number of other IP rights, the most important of which are Database rights and Trade secrets (covered by the law of Privacy and Confidentiality, and Data Protection laws). Many trade secrets are licensed to other businesses to use, often as part of a franchise or licence in conjunction with a patent or other proprietary information. Their disclosure must be tightly controlled because once the information is out in the public domain, it is no longer protected as a trade secret. In addition, there are IP rights in geographic indicators, or GI's, which are signs used on products much like trade marks, however, they are only reserved for products which have a specific origin and possess qualities that are unique to that origin, like Champagne or Greek Yoghurt.

IP Value

That IP adds value to a business is worth mentioning, and is generally well understood by business leaders although actually valuing IP is a subject of huge complexity. So I will be brief here.

Although in the last twenty-five years IP has been recognised as an asset class, it suffers from the fact that it is an intangible, and intangibles are not part of the profit and loss accounts. So, they do not feature on the balance sheet. It is difficult to get them on the balance sheet, although not impossible. Research and development or similar expenses do appear on the balance sheet, though, as do brands that have been acquired. In that case they undergo a formal valuation before being added into the accounts.

Any explanation of IP valuation inevitably gives rise to a discussion about accounting practices and these details make for complexity.

Another issue which makes the subject complicated is that valuation models often require an analysis of what income the IP is generating, which involves first breaking down the income of the business as a whole in order to see which elements of it come from IP.

The fundamental issue to take on board about IP value is that it generally depends on having a successful business.

So, if someone starts a business, registers a trade mark, and then goes bust, the trade mark is unlikely to have any value to speak of. However, if the business becomes a huge success, then its trade mark will have significant value because the brand name will have pulling power (goodwill), and this ability to attract business is valuable.

Just think of the name Coca-Cola, and it should be clear that if you produce a fizzy cola drink and give it a new name, it will be far more difficult to sell it than if you could put the name Coca-Cola on the bottle.

If you have invented something important and have a strong patent over it which others are less able to find a way around, the opportunities to commercialise your IP are going to be more valuable than if you have a patent over something that few people are interested in, or which does not effectively create a barrier to entry for competitors.

To some extent the value of IP might lie in the thing itself, such as a patented invention. Its value will increase when it is marketed well and run as part of a successful business.

Whilst success is not guaranteed on account of a registered IP right, registration of a right does enable the holder to capitalise on the maximum market value inherent to the product in question.

In brief therefore, IP increases a company's value, and an element of that value is down to the exclusivity that your IP gives you.

Exclusivity adds value

IP invariably gives you exclusive rights over something. Its rationale is to give you the right to stop others encroaching on your territory. That is why, like land, it is called 'property'.

With land, if you own a plot it means you can stop others building, or otherwise trespassing on it. Some plots are more desirable than others because of their location and aspect. They will therefore be more sought after and valuable.

IP is similar. It creates scarcity due to the exclusive rights embodied in it.

Just as with land, it is important to take the right steps in order to have valuable IP. For example, if you grant an exclusive right to someone else to reside on your land you will have given away the right to use it, and its value as an asset will be reduced. So, it is with IP.

If you don't take the right steps with IP (which may, for example, involve making good choices when naming products and services) you will not own such valuable IP even if you have a successful business. That may be because the name you choose cannot be exclusive to you.

Owning IP also involves securing your ownership (which is about registration of rights, as well as using the right contracts, or complying with privacy and other laws).

Strategic decisions about IP should be made early in the business so as to identify what IP to create, which rights to register and when. Understanding IP involves knowing how best to exploit the IP so as to not give it away unknowingly, by, for example, sharing your innovations with others before you've had a chance to consider whether they're protectable.

If you have ambitions to succeed and scale your business, you will have IP issues to take on board, and the best way to do that is to have an IP audit and take a strategic approach. This is how you avoid wasting resources and having to undo past actions.

However, what often gets in the way of that is the misinformation that exists around IP law, and the failure by many organisations to understand that the digital economy has changed the rules. In the meantime, there are many myths around IP which I will now briefly consider.

Dangerous views about IP

A common misconception is that IP is all about patents. People justify ignoring IP because they don't have '£50,000 plus to spend on patenting'. While it's true that securing a patent may be optional or may not be worth the investment, at other times it may be the essential protection, without which a business should not operate.

There are other IP rights apart from patents. For example, copyright is the critical IP on which a tech business needs to focus.

The right action for one business will differ enormously from another because much depends on the context, the business concept and vision.

Some business advisers acknowledge the importance of IP for a business producing physical products, or to a business that is already successful and established, or to businesses operating in the creative sector.

Digital IP is foundational

I strongly believe that IP is the foundation of any business and needs early attention by all businesses with ambition. A digital IP lawyer should be the first port of call for anyone developing a new product or service online or which involves commissioning software or other technology.

It is concerning that even those who should know better, such as investors and business advisers misunderstand IP, and sometimes advise others about IP based on their own misconceptions. One myth is that IP is only relevant to an IP-rich business.

Whether due to wrong assumptions about IP involving costly registrations, or ideas as to the expense involved in taking IP advice, IP is often inadequately considered when new ideas are implemented.

A serious error is the belief that IP is all about the protection of what you already have. The message to take on board is that you need expert IP help when deciding how to implement your idea because the choices you make at that stage – of images, names, designs and more – are all IP decisions. The very choice determines whether or not you create something distinctive that is protectable and capable of enhancing its potential value if the underlying business or product is a success. So a good name for your business or product is essentially one to which your target market will be drawn and that is legally effective and available. You would be starting your business on the wrong footing to get so attached to a name that you're not willing to drop it if it transpires that someone else has a better right to it.

Your business needs a contract when it commissions someone to create something like a website, to ensure your interests are protected, and that you will own the IP, or have appropriate permissions to use it in the ways you plan.

It may well be inconvenient for a start-up to stop to take IP advice given how everything else is so easily accessible. You can go online to form a company, buy domains, get the information and templates you need, so pausing to first get IP advice may seem unnecessary.

However, if you're an ambitious business, taking IP advice should be your first step once you have an idea. It should come well before you're ready to actually start your business. Deciding not to take digital IP issues on board from the beginning is gambling with your future. It is not a calculated risk. Risks you accept in business should be well considered and balanced. Ignoring IP is a big risk as this book explains.

That's why we need more education on IP in society. There should be more books, courses and entrepreneurship groups for everyone, including for lawyers.

Possibly a time will come when artificial intelligence produces a cognitive tool to enable initial IP legal issues to be automatically addressed online without the need to actually speak to a lawyer. Until then, you will want to find a digital IP lawyer to advise you on the full range of IP rights and digital issues so you can formulate the right IP strategy.

Conclusion

Everyone should take IP issues on board in their business because the internet has an impact on all businesses, whether they have a website or not, because conversations are taking place on social media all the time about their industry, and possibly about them too, whether they participate or not.

As a buyer of legal services, you may be interested to find out what changes are taking place in the legal industry that could affect you.

So, in the next chapter I will look at the recent deregulation to explain why the legal 'Big Bang' affects you.

Visit *http://azrights.com/ip-revolution-ch1* to take our IP test to assess your IP protection.

Chapter 2

Changing Legal Landscape, and More-for-less Challenge in Law

There is no doubt that the legal profession is on the brink of huge change. This impacts clients of law firms.

The law is fundamentally about knowledge and information. The fact that the web makes information freely available therefore has a deep impact on the legal industry and its business model.

That the web has revolutionised society is undisputed. Yet the digital revolution is still in its infancy, and the new communications it enables are already proving more significant than previous revolutionary developments like the printing press, the telephone, and the television. This is discussed in more depth in the Appendix.

When I was an LLM student in the mid-90s, I read Richard Susskind's book *The Future of the Law* and could not put it down. I was absorbed by its views about legal services and technology and the changes that were on the horizon. For example, he predicted that email would become the main way that lawyers would communicate with their clients. This was at a time when email was an emerging technology.

Soon afterwards I started working at a large international City firm, and suggested we include a provision in our standard boilerplate contracts to allow for notice to terminate by email. The partner in charge dismissed this out of hand because at the time email was considered unusable by law firms due to its security and confidentiality risks. How things have changed.

Naturally I have been a keen follower of Richard Susskind's thinking ever since. He is the oracle for law firms looking for inspiration on handling the combined effect of the web and the Legal Services Act 2007 on legal practice.

Legal Services Act

The Act marks the beginning of a significant transformation in the way legal services are provided to consumers. It implemented Lord Clementi's recommendations for deregulating the legal market so as to make the law more accessible.

It does this in a number of ways, including the allowing of law firms and other businesses to apply for a licence to operate as 'alternative business structures' (ABS).

The ABS is designed to foster more innovative ways of meeting consumer demand for legal services by enabling more efficient and cost effective services for consumers.

While the provision of legal services has traditionally been an activity reserved to qualified practitioners, the new ABS structure allows non-lawyers to have an equity stake in law firms subject to a 'fitness to own' test as to ownership and management. External ownership of a law firm can be 100%. However, all ABSs must have a solicitor as a Compliance Officer for Legal Practice (COLP).

It is generally believed that non-lawyer owners of law firms will cause a sea change in the way legal services are provided. Some law firms will be floated on the stock market in future, and Gateley is the first to have done so in 2015.

The provisions of the Act came into effect at the end of 2011. Although, before its introduction the Act was much discussed as a legal Big Bang, it did not in fact have a significant impact when it was first introduced. One writer even referred to it as a Damp Squib. Some of the earliest ABSs were small law firms that wanted to give a shareholding to a non-lawyer, such as a husband, wife or practice manager.

The legislation is generally regarded as likely to have a significant impact on the legal industry in the long-run once the new providers enter the market.

Law firms were already under pressure from the changes the web had caused. This was magnified by the combination of the recession, the oversupply of law firms, and the new entrants to the legal market who were getting ready to apply to become ABSs. On top of that the Solicitors Regulation Authority's new 'outcomes focused' regulatory landscape increased the costs of compliance for law firms.

Although it is still unclear how the introduction of multidisciplinary practices (MDPs), able to provide businesses with a comprehensive range of services incorporating guidance on legal issues alongside commercial solutions, will change the landscape of legal services, there is no doubt that it will augur significant change for all types of law firm.

Even before obtaining ABS status, big corporates were providing fixed fee offerings in competition with law firms. Examples include More Than, and Barclays, which packaged up the legal and accounting space – offering employment agreements and such like to business clients. They offered these solutions by outsourcing to law firms. Now they can own their own law firms.

The first to suffer from these changes initially has been the high street law firm doing general practice work like conveyancing, probate, wills, and similar. Even before the impact of new competitors many firms have closed down due to the twin pressures of high professional indemnity insurance, and recession. There have also been a few large law firm casualties too, such as Halliwells and Cobbetts.

Although niche firms have fared better, no law firm is immune. The very increase in choice and competition in the market for consumers is bound to have an impact on every type of law firm.

Other industries

It is instructive to look at how Specsavers has emerged out of the deregulation of the opticians' industry. It offers a choice of designer frames for prescription glasses which is a far cry from the days before deregulation when there was little choice for patients visiting opticians who dispensed NHS prescription glasses. What used to be a dominant part of the business – eye testing – is now a tiny element of a business whose understanding of customer needs has led to a focus on choice of frames at cost effective prices.

However, although it is possible to draw parallels between deregulation of the opticians market and legal services by looking at the long term effects of the changes in that industry, it is important to remember that the legal services market is much more complex than the comparators such as optometrists.

Unlike glasses, legal services consist of many different types of services and law firm. There are large city firms, niche practices operating in different areas of the law (for example, pensions, education, IP, corporate, employment and more), general high street practices, legal aid firms, and virtual ('dispersed') law firms. So, it is difficult to generalise about how law firms might respond. In many ways the possibilities depend on the subject area. The sort of extra-legal services that an IP law firm might offer will differ substantially to those a family law firm would contemplate. These will probably have more in common with disciplines related to the specialism than with each other.

It is possible that in future we will see some firms replaced by industry specific integrated firms, for example offering the full range of services that clients of the Healthcare sector might need, such as IP, regulatory guidance, insurance etc. with law being just one element among other disciplines.

Legal Advice Models

Susskind emphasises the need to introduce technology in order to provide value for money services. In his books he develops his theme of standardisation and commoditisation, and expresses the view that what lawyers currently do can be undertaken more quickly, more conveniently and less expensively, and in a less forbidding way, by systems than by conventional legal work.

He cites document assembly, personalised alerting, online dispute resolution, and open-sourcing as examples of 'disruptive legal technologies' in that they do not support or complement current legal practices, but challenge and replace them.

There are various solutions on offer. At one end of the scale there is high cost legal services – the traditional model, where clients pay for a bespoke, personal, easy to access legal service – and at the other end of the scale is an impersonal, do it yourself type service consisting of simple legal documents, either in the form of paper kits or delivered via a software/web interface.

Another theme Susskind picks up is that non-lawyer investors in law firms are not going to be committed to the ways of the past. They are likely to be introducing call centres, outsourcing to India, online legal services, the automatic generation of documents, and more. He concludes that the delivery of legal services will be a very different business when financed and managed by these non-lawyers.

Susskind is right in thinking that it is improbable investors would choose to put cash into the traditional business model of most law firms – hourly billing, expensive premises, pyramidal organisational structures, and the rest.

More-for-less challenge

The recession exacerbated shifts that were already due to occur, and has brought about what is called the more-for-less challenge for law firms.

This stems from the fact that in-house departments had tended to set up bigger and bigger internal teams to handle more of their own legal work, more cost effectively than would be possible if they engaged external law firms. However, General Counsel of these legal departments are under pressure from their management to reduce headcounts and costs. At the same time the amount of legal and compliance work is on the rise.

The increasing amounts of regulation that companies must deal with within our complex world means that companies are finding the cost of legal assistance to support them too expensive. The traditional forms of charging by law firms are now unacceptable for such routine, low level work. So, General Counsel are demanding more legal services at less cost from law firms.

Hourly rate billing does not necessarily deliver value, yet law firms have resisted making such a deep change to their business models, with the result that new entrants to the market have profited.

Many of the larger law firms are having to meet the more-for-less challenge because General Counsel are cutting their budgets, and putting pressure on them to provide more value for money. This inevitably means not charging by the hour for certain types of legal work, and providing a fixed price for the work regardless of how much time will be spent.

Given that the market is increasingly unwilling to tolerate expensive lawyers for certain tasks of guiding, advising, drafting, researching, problem-solving and more, firms are investing in smart systems and processes, and making greater use of paralegals and law graduates located in regional offices. 'North shoring', the practice of setting up offices in less expensive locations than the south east, is on the rise because office space costs half the amount firms pay in central London. Some firms are also outsourcing part of their operations to India. The larger firms set up their own presence in countries such as South Africa and India.

The continuing pressure on legal fees, the scope of SRA regulations, and consequent search by firms to find more cost effective solutions, is bound to lead to ABS firms entering the legal services market as full-blooded providers, as opposed to simply offering a branded referral service, which the likes of Barclays are doing at present.

These companies have the infrastructure, or access to it, through their banking, financial and insurance services arms. Bearing in mind their probable advertising budgets to compete with law firms, it will likely be just a matter of time before perception is gradually shifted as to the natural choice to handle your various legal requirements.

Currently, you are more favourably disposed to solicitors than is commonly believed, particularly when compared to alternative providers. The natural and automatic response to any problem or issue or situation of a legal nature is: 'I need a solicitor to sort this', and this reflects a deeper, implicit belief that only a solicitor can sort it and no-one else is to be trusted.

But in earlier times, solicitors used to be trusted business advisers that you turned to for tax advice, but you probably now think of accountants for general tax advice. So, although nobody knows what will happen with ABS, the challenge for law firms is to stay in the top of the mind of clients seeking legal services.

Meeting customer needs

The challenge in the foreseeable future is how to better meet the needs of you, the customer. Technology solutions are part of the answer. Every element of human involvement that can be digitised will lower the costs of legal services, and therefore, go a long way towards meeting the more-for-less challenge.

Now that the ABS structure enables law firms to offer wider services, every firm must identify the needs of clients, so as to offer them in a timely manner. This involves the consideration of wider services, too.

For example, should an IP firm offer branding and web development services? This is something I considered and rejected because we are all about law, not design or web development. We can add far more value to SMEs by sticking to law. By collaborating with other professionals, such as branding and advertising agencies we would ensure that a wider range of SMEs are supported in their innovation efforts, can commercialise their knowledge, and receive a quality brand.

Our values are based on the assertion that no SME should be without IP advice. We are about making IP accessible for every business – it is not just for the elite.

The ABS regulations allow us to access wider IP-related services. For example, SMEs told Lord Hargreaves (who was commissioned by the Government a few years ago to consider the extent to which digital laws could be reformed) that they would like help with commercialisation. So, a possibility is to set up a separate consultancy division to offer clients services related to IP, such as IP valuation, monetisation, royalty rate determination, damages/loss of profits assessments, and strategic IP portfolio planning, among other things.

While it is not necessary to be an ABS in order to provide the full range of IP and other legal services, only ABSs are able to offer a stake in the business to non-lawyers such as commercialisation specialists, accountants or other non IP professionals who might have a lot to add to a legal practice.

ABSs are an ideal vehicle for introducing innovations to provide the wider range of client services that the market needs. The rationale behind the Act was to reduce complexity for clients.

For now though, it is arguable that the complexity has been increased. For example, I was unable to find a database listing all ABS firms because there are several licensing bodies. So, when you see a company that offers the same services as a law firm, and which refers to their legal staff as lawyers, it is difficult to check them out. The SRA only lists ABS firms that it has licensed itself. If an ABS is licensed by another body such as IPREG or ICAEW, it seems you would need to know which body licensed the particular entity in order to check the relevant list of ABSs of that body.

This makes it difficult for the public to tell a regulated business from a non-regulated one. If you can't readily verify whether an entity is indeed licensed as an ABS, how can you tell a genuine ABS from a business that is not licensed to practice law?

In this climate the scope for confusion is quite high. If I, as a solicitor with some knowledge of what is going on, can't easily work out whether a company is an ABS or is misleading the public, how are members of the public to know what to look out for?

I hope these issues will be ironed out in the near future, and in the meantime, as mentioned already, I think we can best help SMEs and potential agency collaborators by making it easy for them to access the legal services they need.

Conclusion

Increasingly, all law firms are under pressure to deliver more value.

An increased use of IT, along with better management and supervision of lower level staff, are key ways in which the client can expect to receive superior quality legal services at more affordable rates.

Visit *http://azrights.com/ip-revolution-ch2* to see a list of bodies authorised to license ABS entities.

Chapter 3

Solicitors, Barristers, Trade mark, and Patent Attorney Professions

The legal principles governing Intellectual Property and Intellectual Property Rights have evolved over centuries. The Statute of Monopolies (1624) and the British Statute of Anne (1710) are seen as the origins of patent and copyright law respectively.

Despite this, the term 'intellectual property' did not enter into general use until the 1980s. When I was at university in the late 70s, the words used in our text book to describe intangible property were 'choses in action'.

Emergence of specialist patent profession

As far back as 1450, patents were being granted in Venice, mostly in the field of glass-making. There was also much patent-related activity during the industrial revolution in the 19th century as the world transitioned from hand-production methods to machines. New chemical manufacturing and iron-production processes were conceived, and improvements made to water power.

The rationale behind patents and intellectual property rights is that they encourage innovation and investment. So, it is not surprising that these new manufacturing processes and the increasing production of steam power and factory-made machine tools resulted in a number of patents and patent disputes, and called for professionals well-versed in the subject matter of the technologies of the age.

With increasing complexity comes specialisation, so inevitably the new professional discipline of patent agent emerged in the period 1820 to 1840.

A few unscrupulous agents who took money from clients for patents which they never obtained gave the profession a poor reputation initially. So regulation, in the form of the Patent Law Amendment Act of 1852, was passed to deal with and eliminate malpractice.

Regulated providers of IP services

It is important to understand the market today so as to know the difference between the various professionals, and to ensure you only use regulated providers listed on the registers of their professional bodies, namely:

1. The Law Society for solicitors.

2. The Bar Council for barristers.

3. ITMA (Institute of Trade Mark Attorneys) for trade mark attorneys.

4. CIPA (Chartered Institute of Patent Attorneys) for patent attorneys.

A benefit of dealing with a regulated provider is that you have the legal protections of insurance and oversight of an independent third party if there are any problems, such as if the advice you receive turns out to be incorrect.

Solicitors and Barristers

The regulated IP professions include solicitors and barristers who specialise in IP law.

In most countries around the world, in order to practise law it is necessary to have a law degree or its equivalent, to have passed exams and served in an apprenticeship.

Traditionally solicitors have dealt with legal matters in court while barristers did courtroom advocacy, drafted legal pleadings and gave expert legal opinions. Solicitors have more direct access to clients and do transactional legal work, while barristers are rarely hired by clients directly but instead are retained (or instructed) by solicitors to act on behalf of clients.

Changes following deregulation

Deregulation has introduced a number of changes so that the main essential difference between solicitors and barristers in England and Wales today is that solicitors are attorneys, which means that they can act in the place of their client for legal purposes, and may conduct litigation on their behalf by making applications to the court, writing letters in litigation to the client's opponent, and so on.

A barrister, on the other hand, is not an attorney and is forbidden from 'conducting' litigation. This means barristers can only speak on their clients' behalf in court. They may not file court papers. So, those barristers who do take clients on directly must be instructed through a solicitor or other qualified professionals, such as a trade mark attorney or patent agent, as these professionals or the client themselves must file the court papers. Few barristers are currently offering their services directly to the public.

The emergence of the separate discipline of Trade mark Attorney

In the early days of the industrial revolution there were just patent agents as a profession. The separate profession of trade mark attorney emerged later, probably when in the 1930s a group of patent agents split away from the rest of the profession. They left to set up their own professional body, now known as the Institute of Trade Mark Attorneys.

Trade mark and Patent Attorneys

Today in the UK, therefore, trade mark and patent attorneys are two separate, recognised legal professions.

A trade mark attorney is qualified to act in matters involving trade mark law and practice and to provide legal advice on trade mark matters, while a patent attorney has specialist qualifications to represent clients in patents. Both professions have rights of audience before intellectual property courts, although their right to appear in court is limited to trade mark or patent matters.

Other Countries

In the USA, specialists in IP are simply members of the general legal profession that specialise in trade marks. Trade mark attorneys do not sit additional exams, and are part of the general legal profession.

Patent attorneys need an appropriate qualification in a science or engineering field and are required to pass a special exam in order to practise in the United States Patent Office.

In Europe, the harmonisation legislation means that the rights of individuals to practise will stem from their national legal systems; if an individual is entitled to practise in their own country then they will be entitled to practise throughout the EU.

On the other hand, to practise as patent attorney before the European Patent Office (EPO) – a body that exists mainly to grant European patents and to hear and determine third-party challenges to the validity of European patents in opposition proceedings – would depend on whether the individuals are general legal practitioners, such as solicitors, or not. Trade mark and patent attorneys are not 'lawyers' as far as the EPO rules are concerned, meaning that patent attorneys can only represent clients before the EPO if they have passed additional exams to qualify as European Patent Attorneys, while solicitors may practise without need of further exams.

Note that the EPO is not legally bound to the European Union, and exists as a result of the European Patent Convention.

Non-regulated providers

There are, then, other providers of IP services such as IP valuation, IP commercialisation, and registration services, who are unregulated and unqualified. There is no requirement to be a qualified professional in order to search the IP registers, register IP rights or value IP, or help businesses to commercialise IP.

So it's important to be on the alert when engaging the services of IP professionals. That is not to say that non-regulated businesses are not to be used. Some are very professional and experienced in what they do. It's just that there are also many unscrupulous or inexperienced companies and individuals out there. The industry inevitably attracts its fair share of rogues who prey on naive inventers whose hopes and dreams of untold riches as a result of their inventions and ideas make them vulnerable.

As an aside, it is worth noting that solicitors may only provide advice to the public if they act through a regulated law firm. If an employer is not listed against their name on the Law Society's register (the entry will say 'main role not specified'), this means they are not regulated as individual sole practitioners, nor are they employed by an entity that is licensed to give advice to the public. You would have none of the protections you get when using a sole practitioner or solicitor employed by a regulated provider when engaging their services. Indeed, engaging the services of a solicitor directly without involving their employer means you get none of the protections, such as insurance, that you otherwise have.

Some solicitors are unwittingly breaching the rules by providing legal services directly to the public through their own companies believing that they are entitled to do so because they are not providing "reserved" activities. However, I know one high profile solicitor who provides software services through a separate business, who has been told by the SRA that his software business is effectively providing 'advice'. This is considered to be an activity reserved solely to solicitors. So, the SRA's argument is that his separate business is breaching the rules.

At the time of writing the separate business rule is being revised, so it will be interesting to see if the SRA makes it clearer in future whether or not giving advice is a reserved activity. Currently there are many solicitors who are operating on the assumption that they may practise law through an ordinary company while maintaining their practising certificate.

The fact that quite a few solicitors are now running businesses in breach of the rules and advising clients without the benefit of professional indemnity insurance is testament to the complexity of the regulations.

Division of responsibilities between trade mark attorneys and solicitors

Historically, IP solicitors provided strategic advice, litigation services, and specialist copyright expertise, while trade mark attorneys specialised in trade mark registration work. Solicitors would pass such work on to trade mark attorneys, and in return received copyright advisory or litigation referrals from trade mark attorneys.

Barristers would be instructed to draft court pleadings and appear as advocates in court.

Ten years ago these distinctions began to break down. Today, an increasing number of law firms file trade marks themselves instead of passing the work to firms of trade mark attorneys, and many of them have established substantial trade mark practices as a result. Some firms employ trade mark attorneys on their teams, while others register trade marks without involving trade mark attorneys. Many firms also offer patent registration services, although they will universally engage the services of specialist patent attorneys in order to do so.

On the other hand, many patent and trade mark attorney firms now conduct litigation work themselves and do not refer the work to solicitors. The rules allow them to do so. Many of the larger trade mark and patent attorney firms have gone on to set up their own separate law firms employing solicitors to deal with litigation, copyright, drafting agreements and much more.

Competition between trade mark attorneys and solicitors

The training to qualify as a solicitor is considered adequate to equip a solicitor to go on to practise in any area of the law without the need for further exams. So if you're using a solicitor who specialises in IP law, they're likely to have picked up the subject through practical experience. Some solicitors will have studied IP law at Master's degree level.

It's not uncommon for solicitors to have also taken the specialist trade mark attorney exams, so that they are dual qualified as solicitors and trade mark attorneys. I myself attended the trade mark attorney course in order to study trade mark law in more depth. However, I decided against taking their exams because qualifying as a trade mark attorney was not important to me. I felt I'd done enough exams to last me a lifetime.

When David Clementi reviewed regulation of the professions, his final recommendations proposed a more unified regulatory system. So new structures for cross-professional work were enshrined in the Legal Services Act 2007, and all these professionals were classed as 'lawyers'. Previously only solicitors and barristers were lawyers.

Is the UK Intellectual Property Office guiding you correctly?

When choosing a lawyer, it is good to understand more about the firm and how its relevant department operates rather than assuming that its brand name automatically assures quality in every area.

Because in most countries there is the view that general legal practitioners are qualified to practise in any field of law without the need to take additional exams to those required to enter the legal profession, this has led to some lawyers doing work in which they have no experience.

Intellectual property is deemed, by the professional indemnity insurers, to be a high risk activity for solicitors to dabble in, and the Intellectual Property Office alerts the public to only use a solicitor who is experienced in IP. The website warns the public to only use experienced solicitors, and seems to encourage you to use trade mark attorneys rather than solicitors.

However, now that the requirement not to dabble in areas in which a solicitor is not well versed is enshrined in the Solicitors Regulation Authority's conduct regulations, it is arguably less likely that a solicitor would undertake IP work without experience.

There is a lot more to IP than registering patents, and trade marks. It is unlikely that SMEs would get the right range of IP advisory support by going to a firm of trade mark attorneys in preference to a firm of digital IP lawyers.

Why the current system is broken

It's important that Government organisations are able to put you in touch with the right type of law firm to handle your needs.

Why does the Intellectual Property Office website direct the public to trade mark attorneys then? Surely, the IPO should be highlighting that IP involves a lot more than trade marks and mentioning the relevance of an IP/IT law firm for tech or online businesses? This illustrates how society has not yet caught up with the changed needs of SMEs.

The Intellectual Property Office (IPO) in the UK is charged with spreading information about intellectual property, although the Government does not provide it with adequate funding and resources to do so. The IPO derives an income from UK trade mark filings, which meant that during the recession the office had to lay off 100 staff because trade mark filings dropped markedly.

The IPO does a really good job despite its stretched resources. However, one downside to putting the Office in charge of raising awareness of IP is that this tends to reinforce the impression that IP is all about registration of trade marks, designs and patents.

Currently, SMEs leave IPO workshops assuming they must register a trade mark. Many of these are start-ups who then go on to register their own trade marks, often registering quite inappropriate names, or wasting their resources by making several attempts because they receive no professional help. For example, they register purely descriptive terms with a logo, failing to appreciate that this gives them little protection in return for committing much of their limited resources.

So the current system of professional specialisation whereby the UK Intellectual Property Office's website directs you to trade mark attorneys for your naming needs, doesn't make it easy for you to go straight to the optimum help you need. You are expected to find a commercial law firm that can meet your other IP requirements; in practice, other commercial legal issues, such as copyright, fall between the cracks and remain unaddressed for many businesses.

Ideally, if more companies emerge to offer one-stop-shop IP services, you will have the convenience of accessing skills in one place, and the professional divisions between types of lawyer would not get in the way of that.

In the meantime, it is inappropriate to expect you to have to visit several different types of law firm to access the range of expertise your business needs. Maybe if you visit an accountant for your start-up, you never go on to visit a solicitor or trade mark or patent attorney because your accountant might set you up with a company, register your trade mark even, and possibly even give you some templates. The accountant is unlikely to identify a need to refer you to a digital or any other type of IP specialist unless you have an obvious need, like for patent advice.

One of my aims in writing this book is to publicise the reason start-up businesses should be directed to a lawyer for digital IP help. A general commercial law firm is unlikely to have the detailed understanding of IP and IT law that is required in today's business environment so it is not easy to find the full range of IP specialist skills you need. And firms of trade mark attorneys do not usually offer the digital IP services you need.

The entire rationale of the Legal Services Act was to make access to legal services more convenient for the client. Yet the current landscape is more confused than ever.

Conclusion

Although the Legal Services Act was designed to make it all much easier for you to access the legal services you need, and to have them packaged up with other useful related services, in the short term the situation has been made incredibly complicated. The existence of so many different classes of lawyer is exacerbating the situation.

As I will explain in the next chapter, start-ups are particularly losing out in this scenario, and failing to get the help they really need.

Visit *http://azrights.com/ip-revolution-ch3* for links to websites of the various professional bodies, and guidance on how to identify whether your legal professional is a qualified solicitor.

Part Two

Central Relevance of IP in a Digital World

Chapter 4

Start-ups in a Digital World

The right lawyer to advise your business in the digital world will be one with a good understanding of the web and technology. The range of topics on which you need advice are indicated in this book, with some highlights reviewed in this chapter.

Given the widespread ownership of smartphones and the trends towards a sharing economy, peer-to-peer lending, crowd-funding, use of big data, apps, and more, the business landscape necessarily means your lawyer should understand the online dimension. Indeed, the technological advancements that are transforming our lives mean that the web will be the only facet of many businesses.

So your lawyer needs to stay abreast of new developments and emerging technologies in order to advise not just on the law and legal documentation, but also on other aspects of doing business online.

Opportunities created by the web

As well as causing huge upheaval, the web has brought with it opportunities for entrepreneurial people.

Start-ups which were once limited to marketing to a local audience are now able to market their products and services worldwide, and the costs of setting up and running a business have been vastly reduced.

It is possible to create very substantial businesses from simple ideas – for example, Uber and Airbnb. However, unless you have a good grasp of how IP impacts your online business or software needs, you could suffer setbacks in the ways outlined in this book. Implementing your idea into an online solution requires skills in technology, and good IP help.

No need for physical presence

Before the web it was much more important for companies to have physical trading premises which customers could visit, such as a high street store. The web provides a more cost effective way to market and sell your products to customers. You can postpone obtaining office space till your concept is proven, or never need it at all.

It has never been easier for people with an idea to set up in business. You just need a website or blog and can use social media to promote your new business concept. Whether you want to create an enduring business that someone else will one day buy, or just want to test your ideas in a low cost way, the web gives you the possibility to market your ideas to a global audience.

There is always the potential online to differentiate yourself by creating an offering which sets you apart.

These two case studies may give you an idea of how some businesses have not only differentiated themselves from their competitors but have also disrupted the conventional framework in which they operate.

Nutmeg

Nutmeg is an online investment management start-up whose premise is simple: to enable customers to invest manageable amounts of money into a portfolio of assets, including equities, bonds and commodities. Traditionally such investment has been reserved for those who understand the markets well enough to trade themselves, or else others who command the required money to attract the services of a stockbroker or private banker.

Nutmeg decides how to invest its customers' money based on their personal profiles - taking into consideration factors such as risk and timescale - and thus empowers the individual, regardless of respective wealth.

Nutmeg is just one example of the opportunities that exist to disrupt your market through the provision of online services. Sometimes a few small tweaks to the business model made possible by the web can bring about fundamental changes to the established ways of doing things.

Uber

Consider Uber – it is essentially a technology platform which makes it easy for the public to use self-employed car drivers as cabs in order to undercut the standard taxi fare. Despite the downsides of using unlicensed cab drivers who are reliant on a satnav to navigate them, the service has been a roaring success.

Aside from being highly innovative service offerings that bridge a variety of different target consumers, these two successful business models also have an added benefit: data. Whilst the ideas behind Nutmeg and Uber are in themselves great, the sheer amount of data collected, the number of trades, length of taxi routes taken, user ratings etc., helps generate more ideas and intellectual property in such a way that inevitably leads to compounded success.

Nature of legal help needed

You are likely when setting up in business nowadays to need a website, app or other software. There are many legal ramifications here. To achieve a successful outcome, it's essential to involve a lawyer who can advise on them before you commission a third party to do any work for you.

If the project goes wrong, as often happens when technology is commissioned by an entrepreneur without experience of the complexities involved, there is often not enough money at stake to justify litigation. So, your start-up would suffer unnecessary financial losses, not to speak of the loss of time.

Avoiding traps for the unwary

The ease of starting up online is a trap for the unwary. Building a great platform requires much thought and planning, and must involve a competent tech lawyer on the team.

The main reason why people choose a name, buy a domain name and commission a website before consulting a lawyer experienced in IT and IP law is their lack of awareness of the need for early IP advice.

If you are successful in your niche, the value in your business will lie in its intangible assets – your intellectual property – which makes it important to understand the IP issues from the outset.

In the past, people consulted lawyers before setting up a business because they may have needed to rent or buy premises. Nowadays, with so many online company formation businesses competing at low cost, the availability of templates for your business, and office addresses that enable you to work from home while appearing to have a sizeable presence, people inevitably tend to have less access to expert help when setting up in business.

The lack of education about IP in schools and colleges means that some businesses fall into the trap of assuming that just because they flouted copyright rules as students, and freely downloaded copyright infringing material, that the same behaviour is acceptable in business.

Essentially, just as people don't cavalierly commission the building of a house without expert advice, so you should not commission sophisticated websites without legal help.

It's true that you don't always involve a lawyer when you engage an architect. However, architects are a regulated profession. Web design and development is not regulated, so you do not have the legal protections you may need to rely on when you engage an agency to build you a website or software. Legal help will ensure you have proper protection if the project fails to meet your expectations. It will also address key questions concerning the IP rights you need in the platform. This is not something to leave till after you've commissioned a company.

Another situation where you would need legal help is if your new business idea involves setting up a social media platform. You may want to interface with other sites in order to access media such as news, images, music and more. This involves knowing about your legal position when using an application programming interface, or API for short. The law in this area is constantly evolving.

Oracle v Google

This dispute began in 2012, when Google, creator of the Android operating system for mobile telephones, made use of Oracle's Application Programming

Interface (API). Oracle created the Java programming language, and the question concerned whether the API was protected by copyright. If so, then Google was not free to make use of it without Oracle's permission.

To appreciate the implications of the case, a basic understanding of APIs is necessary. Broadly speaking, an API is a language a programmer can use to talk to a system. It has a list of commands which can be issued to it.

For example, the API for a graphics application could include the commands "Draw a rectangle" and "Draw a circle". Two different systems might have a different underlying mechanism for drawing a rectangle, for example, system A might draw a rectangle dot by dot starting from the top left corner, while system B might do it in four steps, drawing each side one line at a time.

Despite these underlying differences, if both systems A and B understand the same set of commands, such as "Draw a rectangle" command, then a piece of software written for system A will also run on system B.

Returning to Google and Oracle, the Java APIs owned by Oracle are sets of commands which can be understood by a whole host of different systems. Their advantage is that there could be no need to write different versions of the same software for different platforms. So, the same app might run just as happily on your Mac as on your PC.

Google, when developing the Android operating system, built it to use the Java APIs. This meant that some existing software could function more easily on their new platform, and many developers were already familiar with Java so could get started writing software for Android without a steep learning curve. Although Java and Android accept the same instructions, the underlying code, by which they execute those instructions, is not the same.

Oracle argued that its Java API was protected by copyright, and that Google was not authorised to use it without permission. Google, on the other hand, argued that the Java APIs are simply a way to work with a system, and should not be protected by copyright.

The US courts initially sided with Google, finding that the Java APIs were not copyrightable. However, upon appeal a federal court overturned the earlier ruling, and said that the APIs were protected by copyright. Google's request to appeal to the Supreme Court was rejected, so that it is now firmly established that in the US APIs are copyright.

The legal position on this side of the Atlantic, however, is not the same.

SAS Institute and World Programming (WPL)

The European Court of Justice held that the functionality of a piece of software, or the programming language it uses, is not protected by copyright. Some commentators have interpreted the case as deciding that APIs are not eligible for copyright protection because this would 'monopolise ideas'.

However, the cases covered quite different issues. Functionality and programming language are not the same as an API. Android and Java are different programming languages but use the same APIs.

When Google initially wanted to use Java, they were unable to do a deal with Sun because they didn't want to pay licence fees. So, they decided to write their own language and base it on Java. To do so they lifted Oracle's API. They didn't merely look at it in order to create their own version without any direct copying, they used the API itself and yet made Android incompatible with Java. By not making Android interoperable, they cut out one of the defences that might otherwise have been available to them.

On the basis that we are not comparing like with like when looking at these two cases, it would be interesting to having a ruling from the EU on the same facts. In the meantime, given that most APIs that you might want to use are US-based, in practice the US ruling is the one that you would need to heed if you wanted to use an API.

The upshot is that you may need permission from the owner of a platform if you want to create another system which is compatible with it. For example, if you wanted your social network to be compatible with Facebook apps, you would need permission from Facebook.

The legal protection of computer software is a complex and fast paced area of law. The take-away message is to bear in mind that you may need permission to create a system which is compatible with existing software.

Websites, apps and software

Websites, apps and other software consist of a whole host of different elements, each of which is protected by different IP rights.

For example, websites are a bundle of software, graphics, audio, data, video and written content, packaged together under a domain name. Many of these could potentially be in different ownership.

Copyright in the underlying code that allows the site to function will be one of the important elements to address, as will the domain name used to find it. Ownership of a domain is contractually vested in the registrant, so company owners should register their own domains instead of leaving this to a web design company or to one of their employees.

In this chapter I focus on websites, as they are common to all modern businesses. However, similar principles apply in the case of an app or other software.

When engaging designers and developers to design and build a website, whether using the help of an established web design business or an individual through an online service such as Elance or PeoplePerHour, it is all too easy to find that a gulf emerges between a company's expectations and the reality of what is delivered. So, it is a good idea to not commission a website too hastily.

Vast sums of money are regularly wasted by start-ups because risks are not properly managed from the outset. A written agreement can be a useful way to manage risks. However, that is just part of the consideration. Understanding the technical issues that impact a software development project can also be key to preventing problems.

The agreement would cover common contractual points such as payment as well as a range of other important issues. IP is one of the most important of these, and I will discuss that in the copyright chapter.

The contract should also clearly define how the project will be managed, what will be delivered and when, and what will happen if certain things go wrong.

Developers might approach projects in different ways so a lawyer who understands website projects can help ensure you are happy with the way your developers work.

If you have given the project a lot of thought, and have a clear idea of the outcome you are hoping for, then it may be best to describe the details of your desired website in a specification. That way you would avoid misunderstandings over what is, and is not, to be included within the price you agree.

On the other hand, sometimes this approach can be inflexible. For example, if you later change your plans, it may be difficult to agree reasonable costs for the amendments you need.

More modern 'agile' software development practices allow for a continuously evolving specification. This would suit a situation where your initial requirements are less specific as you can get started more quickly. Changes in your priorities as the finished product comes together can also be taken into account without protracted negotiation or significant expense, although you may need to sacrifice one feature to allow for another if you want to remain within your budget.

Taking the time to agree terms will save you trouble in the long run, and leave you with the best chance of getting the website you want. The time to consider longer term issues such as maintenance, support, changing providers, and service levels is also when you're first choosing a developer. Don't leave it as an afterthought.

Content management

Websites should be easy to maintain. A content management platform enabling you to add material and make basic changes yourself is essential. And think about what would happen if you needed to change the layout, or add new features. How will your developer charge you? How quickly can you expect a response?

If you decide to switch to another developer, what will be involved? From a legal perspective you need the right to get a third party to adapt the website. However, from a practical point of view, it will be easier to engage someone else if the technology which is used for the website is a popular one, such as WordPress.

Where your developer builds your website on its own proprietary platform it may be difficult to outsource to another supplier in future. On the other hand, if they use a common content management system such as WordPress which has a large community of developers, it will be easier to source alternative help later on.

Support

If your website, app or software delivers a service to your customers, or is otherwise business critical, your support and availability needs will depend on your particular business needs.

Some of the assurances you might need include that your website will be accessible 24/7, particularly if it is international (it is not uncommon to agree to 99.9% availability); that if there is a problem there will be someone on hand to fix it quickly; that sufficient bandwidth and processing power will be available to service a large volume of visitors; that regular backups are made and reasonable security precautions are taken to prevent loss of data; and that your site will be compatible with all modern browsers, and will be 'responsive' so it looks appealing on mobile devices. Typically, these will be set out in a service level agreement or 'SLA'.

If you are using a third party to host your website, you will also have a contract with them.

Hosting requirements may be dictated by the functionality you need for your site. For example, will you need a database, video streaming, ecommerce functionality, or a particular platform such as WordPress? If your website deals with personal information consider making it secure, which will involve obtaining an 'SSL' certificate.

The location of your hosting is also important. If you collect information from visitors, then in order to comply with data protection rules you may need to choose a hosting provider whose physical premises are based within the EU.

Documentation

Aside from contracts with suppliers, you also need a range of documentation with end users. These include terms of use to describe how visitors can use your website, ecommerce terms to govern sales to customers, and a privacy policy to comply with data protection rules.

There will be a need for various different terms depending on the business. For example, a social network may want to include the right to suspend or terminate access where a user harasses others through the site, or publishes infringing content. An acceptable use policy is useful to cover such eventualities.

Also, different jurisdictions have different laws. So, if your users are international, you may need to eventually ensure compliance with the regulations of a variety of countries.

Your lawyer needs a good practical understanding of international considerations in order to engage services of lawyers in other key markets to review your materials for local law implications. Similarly, your lawyer should understand the digital environment so as to give you impartial advice on legal matters like use of trade marks in Adwords or other advertising. The legal issues require a good understanding of digital marketing.

How I developed my technical understanding

My knowledge of digital issues has been developed over the years. In the early days I worked closely with software developers at Reuters for five years so acquired a good understanding of technology issues. Since setting up Azrights ten years ago, I've learned a lot more about practical technical issues of web and IT development, partly as a result of involving my husband, Paul Smith, in the business. He had thirty years' experience in IT working on financial systems projects for large pension funds, and helps us on web and IT matters. He also holds a key role in the business as its Compliance Officer for Finance and Administration (COFA).

In 2009 I began to deliver workshops at the Business and IP Centre of the British Library to help start-ups understand what was involved in creating an online brand and business. Paul, my husband, accompanied me on those three hour workshops and provided technical input when members of the audience had IT questions, so his knowledge of IT and web development gradually transferred to me.

There is nothing like teaching a subject to learn it, and a few years of delivering these quarterly workshops gave me clarity about the technology, business, and legal aspects of online business. It also helped me to communicate complex ideas in plain English.

So, digital IP – that is the practical aspects of websites, software, branding, domain names, copyright, social media, online marketing and more – became an important focus of mine and that of Azrights. The workshop content culminated in my first book, *Legally Branded*, which was published in 2012.

Azrights has always attracted staff with formal or informal backgrounds in computer science, as these lawyers tend to be passionate about working in our area of specialism – IP with a strong digital bias.

Conclusion

The arrival of the web and digital technologies which gave rise to the social web has impacted the type of business advice companies need. If your lawyer works in a firm that can provide wide-ranging digital IP help (including registration services) you will get effective support in the areas outlined in this book for your new business venture.

It's important to appreciate the important business input this advice gives you. Avoid regarding legal help as being only about registration or document drafting. This should be integrated with IP and other advice. There are many reasons the support of a digital IP lawyer would advance your business ideas, and these are outlined throughout this book.

Advising companies in today's tech environment often involves doing so in a context where there is an absence of clear laws to determine how your plans might be impacted. Tech moves faster than the law can keep up with, so a good digital IP lawyer is one who has enough legal and business experience to help you navigate the rules even where there is a legal vacuum.

Visit *http://azrights.com/ip-revolution-ch4* for more information about 'Start-ups and Patent'.

Chapter 5

The Relevance of Copyright in an Information Age

Digitisation makes IP relevant to every business, and this is especially true of copyright because it is universally applicable.

Copyright law was introduced more than 100 years ago to address the problems of the print industry. Works in hard copy and in analogue form were difficult and expensive to reproduce so copyright laws were ideal for enabling artists and authors to more readily restrict the circulation of their works and gain a higher price for them.

However, digitisation has meant that books, sound recordings and recorded music can be reproduced at no cost, and often in identical quality to the original. Similarly, in the field of photography and image production photographs and films can now be stored digitally and reproduced in high quality at a vastly reduced cost.

So the internet has led to a huge increase in piracy of intellectual property, which is again an example of how deeply IP is impacted by the web. Not only is the subject more widely relevant to everyone in the digital age, but its content is also impacted in the case of copyright.

Peer to peer file sharing technology has made it possible for audio and visual files to be widely circulated, in a manner which is very difficult to police.

Content online is not in the public domain

However, this state of affairs should not lead anyone to assume that a cavalier approach to copyright laws is acceptable online.

Contrary to popular belief, content that is on the web is not in the public domain. So, once you are involved in a business, it is important to be careful to not infringe on others' rights when taking images or copying materials you find online. Always look into the rights before putting content on your website or in your blog posts.

At the same time the new web environment makes it much easier for people to discover whether their copyright, designs, or products are being copied. For example, websites such as TinEye or Google's search by image are used by copyright owners to find out where their photos are being used. Similarly, there are sites like Copyscape which can identify whether content is copied elsewhere. So a lack of clarity about the limits of copyright and IP laws could be dangerous for a business.

A business would soon get into trouble if it failed to take heed of what materials it may or may not freely use online.

Start-ups and established businesses alike should take the time to understand copyright law if they are to reduce their exposure to copyright infringement risks.

Copyright Essentials

Although this is not a book about black letter law, it is important to briefly explain some essential points about copyright so you know what copyright does and doesn't protect and, consequently, what material you may use.

Copyright is an IP right underpinning the business models of many industries such as publishing, music, films, technology and digital media. These copyright industries are all facing some unique challenges due to the ease with which their works can be copied.

However, copyright is important to every business, even those that are not in copyright dependent industries, because many commonly used assets which all businesses have, like websites, brochures, and logos are protected by copyright.

Examples of copyright works include:

- books, brochures, letters and contracts
- music and sound recordings
- films and videos
- artistic works, drawings, illustrations and photographs
- logos and packaging
- software and games.

Copyright is primarily governed by contract law, and presents many traps for the unwary due to some popular misconceptions. One is that copyright automatically belongs to the commissioner of a work once they've paid for it.

Another common misconception is that names you choose for your business or products are protected by copyright law. They are not.

Names are not protected by copyright

The right to use a name derives from trade mark law rather than from copyright law.

The decision not to give names the benefit of copyright protection was made in 1982, in a case where Exxon Corp unsuccessfully applied to stop Exxon Insurance Consultants calling themselves Exxon. The company argued that it had copyright in the name because it had spent substantial amounts of money in developing it.

The court disagreed, stating that from a policy point of view it wanted to keep names out of copyright and to use trade marks to determine ownership rights in names.

We will see later in the trade mark chapter that the rights to use a name belong to the person that uses it in their business. Therefore, an agency who helps a business to find a name will not have any rights to the name. Sometimes agencies assume they have rights so to avoid confusion it's important to mention it here.

Basics of contract law

A contract will exist whether there is any signed legal agreement or not. The law implies certain terms into oral contracts, such as over who is to own copyright, and you may not be aware of those terms when you engage someone without a written agreement.

A case involving Innocent Smoothies shows that sometimes a court is likely to regard an unsigned contract which was discussed by the parties as binding between them.

Innocent's recent litigation illustrates this principle well.

Innocent Smoothies

The case concerned ownership of copyright in the well-known Innocent halo logo, to which a company known as Deepend had acquired the rights from the designers. Deepend argued that Innocent did not have the right to use the logo as Deepend had received an assignment of the copyright in the logo from the designers who had created the brand.

At the time the logo was designed, Innocent was a fledgling company who had started a business relationship with the designers. Their brief was to 'develop the "visual identity for the product".' Although the designers never received payment for their design work, the unsigned Heads of Agreement included a provision requiring the designers to transfer copyright to Innocent of any work approved by Innocent. There was an obligation on Innocent to allot shares to the designers. However, the judge found that neither of these requirements were expressed as a conditional obligation.

The judge used a flipped example to make his point, saying that the obligations to allot shares could theoretically arise even if there was no transfer of copyright to Innocent.

This decision, more than anything, highlights the importance of explicitly stating within a contract that IP rights are conditional on remuneration.

Another important lesson from the Innocent dispute is to explicitly agree copyright ownership from the outset in order to avoid costly litigation further down the line.

The fact that the courts are sometimes willing to interpret the details included in an unsigned agreement to achieve a just result should be a warning to ensure the finalisation and signing of your official paperwork.

Another problem with oral contracts is simply that if a dispute arises over what was agreed, it can be messy and expensive to sort out. The litigation process would involve having the lawyers on both sides examine all the minute details to find out who said what and when in order to determine what was actually agreed.

Buyer Beware principle

Whatever transaction you are involved in, the law says 'Buyer beware'.

Where ownership of IP is concerned, it is usually more to your disadvantage as a buyer to not have a written contract than it is for the supplier. That's because the creator of a work automatically owns copyright in it.

So, if you engage a software developer to write software for you and don't use a written agreement to govern the relationship, then under the law the software developer will own copyright. Not having an agreement ensures that the developer retains copyright over something that may contain all your best ideas and insights about a particular business area. They can take it all within their software program and market it to your competitors.

An example of how this can and does happen in real life is the CML case.

Clearsprings Management Limited (CML) and Businesslinx Limited

In 2005, CML came up with a great software idea, and hired a third party to develop it with a view to selling it once completed. There was only one problem. Even though the software was built for CML, ownership of the software remained with the developers, and CML had nothing to sell. They merely had a right to use it internally. Clearsprings had made a classic error which seems to be repeated time and time again. There was a legal agreement, however it failed to address copyright. By entering into an agreement without proper understanding of copyright law meant that the company signed up to an agreement that failed to address the vital issue of copyright ownership. The court implied a licence in favour of Clearsprings to use the software. However, as ownership of the software lay with the developers, Clearsprings did not own any rights in the idea. The practical consequence is that it had nothing to sell, it could only use the software it had commissioned.

Make sure if you're using templates to commission a copyright work that you understand whether the copyright and other IP provisions are appropriate to your plans. If you don't discuss ownership or appropriate licence terms before you're committed to using a particular supplier, you are storing up potential problems for yourself later on. Going back to someone to renegotiate terms when the rights have a value invariably means people will be reluctant to agree to transfer them over to you without further payment. The time to discuss such details is when they want to win the commission.

Avoiding risks when engaging web developers

One IP issue to bear in mind is the importance of ensuring that the agencies, designers, and developers you engage have sufficient understanding of IP law to avoid infringing on other people's names, or copyright materials. Also, check whether they are using appropriate documentation within their business when engaging freelance help, which is a traditional practice in the industry, and impacts the copyright ownership the agency is able to grant to you.

The contract with them provides the ideal opportunity to inform the people whose services you intend to engage about the need to avoid using works owned by third parties without permission.

The next couple of case studies illustrate that it is not uncommon for web designers to make these mistakes, making the business owner liable.

The DARE and Antiquesportfolio cases are a couple of examples among many others of what can go wrong in the course of the development of websites.

Drug Abuse Resistance Education (DARE)

The designer engaged to produce the DARE website found images on a government website depicting various drugs, and assumed they were free to use. DARE took the designer at their word, but it transpired that the photographs were in fact owned by a professional photographer. Having discovered the unauthorised use of his work, the photographer took legal action, and DARE were faced with an award of £10,000 in damages, plus interest.

Antiquesportfolio

The website designer used images from an antiques encyclopaedia without permission. The buyer found out before facing a lawsuit, and refused to pay for the website. The court held that they were within their rights in refusing to pay the designer for the work because the designer had delivered them an infringing site.

These cases demonstrate that you cannot assume your web designers will know what materials and images they may or may not use.

Alternatively, if you're a web designer, you will know to check the position carefully as it could potentially cost you a lot of money to make mistakes over copyright.

It is important to take all precautionary steps when extracting any content from the internet. You need to make sure you are free to use a particular content without recourse.

There are some ways in which you can freely take images and content from the internet; however, these are limited to activities such as reporting, private use, criticism and review as well as studying. If you are using copyright content for commercial purposes and don't own the rights or licence, you run the risk of being liable for damages.

Risks for designers

On the other hand, I've come across instances where designers suffered liability for using images that their clients asked them to use.

An insufficient basic understanding of copyright law meant that one designer exposed herself to potentially devastating liability for infringing on an artist's work when, against her better judgment she used an image her client had found on the internet in her designs for that client.

The image was used on some merchandise. As the web makes it very easy to discover infringing use of content, the artist whose image had been misused soon found out about the infringement, and demanded a hefty sum of money as compensation. This led the company to having to recall hundreds of thousands of products. They also had to compensate the artist.

As the designer is primarily responsible under the law, she was at significant risk. Had her client not paid the damages, she would have been the person responsible for the infringement as she had used the image in the designs. Even winding up her company would not have helped her escape liability in damages as she faced personal liability under the copyright legislation. She could have lost her house.

So, everyone using copyright content needs to take great care to ensure the material is appropriately licensed.

Licensing

If you use someone else's copyright material under a licence, as you would when using stock library images, make sure the terms of the licence permit the use you intend.

A firm grasp of licensing rules, including the Creative Commons licence terms gives you the ability to navigate copyright more safely online. The severe costs involved if a product needs to be recalled, makes proper due diligence essential when using copyright works on a physical product.

Advisers

As mentioned earlier, it has traditionally fallen on solicitors to advise on copyright laws, rather than trade mark and patent attorneys.

At one time the IP world worked broadly along the lines that names were the province of trade mark attorneys, while patent attorneys dealt with innovations that required patenting, and IP solicitors focused on advising copyright dependent industries. Solicitors also conducted litigation of all IP matters, and also drafted legal agreements such as licences and technology transfer contracts that underpin IP.

Everything is changing rapidly in the digital age. For example, patent and trade mark attorney firms have acquired rights of audience to litigate, while many law firms decided to offer trade mark and patent filing services. The old demarcation lines between the professions make it difficult for businesses to know who to turn to for their diverse IP needs.

This state of affairs means you could potentially receive inadequate advice. Say you avail yourself of free IP support that is often on offer at places like the British Library's Business and IP Centre. What is likely to happen is that you will have a consultation with a patent or trade mark attorney on issues like names and patents. Unless you are also directed to an advisor on digital IP issues, you could well end up receiving no legal help with your website or other technology developments unless you are aware of the importance of doing so. Even if you know that you need to consult a digital IP lawyer on copyright and other commercial matters, you may decide not to devote the necessary time, or resources to finding and visiting several different firms. So, the IT and copyright matters could fall between the cracks.

The traditional demarcation between the professions is simply not tenable any more for SME businesses. Insofar as firms only offer trade mark and patent attorney services, or simple commercial law services, you could miss out on the more detailed digital IP advice the new environment calls for.

Digital IP help means also advising you on names rather than leaving names to the trade mark profession. Names often involve wider digital considerations such as domain names, search engine optimisation, and online marketing too. As for companies that don't visit a lawyer at all because they intend to cut costs by buying templates or copying their competitors' terms, they are taking inappropriate risks and should re-evaluate their decision if their business operates in a copyright intensive industry like technology (which includes the web).

Copyright reforms

In recognition of the importance of the web in enabling entrepreneurial activity, the Government commissioned Professor Hargreaves to consider the extent to which digital laws could be reformed so as to make it as possible to proceed with new business models in this country as it is in the USA.

However, despite the subsequent reforms to the law that resulted, the fundamental problem with copyright is that there has been a piecemeal approach to its reform over the last 100 years. This makes it difficult for Hargreaves or any other purely UK initiative to make substantial progress in improving the law. It will probably take an EU wide initiative for radical overhaul of copyright laws to truly rationalise a law that was designed for print.

Copyright law can be complex and fast moving. For example, there has been quite a lot of case law on the simple topic of whether or not you risk infringing copyright when you link to other online content. Although it has now been decided that simple linking (that does not circumvent a pay wall and links to content that is generally already available) does not infringe copyright, there are still areas of uncertainty in the law which make linking potentially risky in certain situations.

If you want to scrape content from other sites in order to create a more convenient platform for potential users to access that type of information in one place – namely on your new platform – or have other plans involving copyright material, you should seek advice to understand and weigh the risks before proceeding with, or abandoning, a project.

Small businesses often approach us expecting to receive a simple answer over the phone as to whether or not their project will be on the right side of the law. They may point to other sites doing something similar and want to know whether their plans will also be alright. They expect to get this advice for free. The law does not lend itself to black and white, yes/no answers in this way. The answer is often going to be, 'it depends on the details of your plans and how you intend to implement your site'.

Due to the complexities of IP law, you should accept the need to invest in advice if you want proper answers to your questions. The tendency to only be willing to pay to have something done, such as a registration or document drafting misses the fact that advice is often the best way your lawyers can add value. The key is to understand what your ideas are, how they exist in a legal framework and more importantly who they belong to, and only then can you expect to properly commercialise them. Similarly, if you want to do something which might infringe on somebody else's rights, the only way to find out if you can overcome those hurdles is to invest in advice.

A successful entrepreneur who understood the importance of IP, and copyright in particular, is Microsoft's Bill Gates. He took care over the rights in the first piece of software Microsoft produced and was careful to ensure he owned the copyright.

Microsoft

When a pre-market copy of Microsoft's BASIC was leaked into the computer hobbyists' community in February 1976 and widely copied and distributed, Gates wrote an open letter to the hobbyists. His letter stated that he (amongst others) could not continue to produce, distribute, and maintain high-quality software without payment.

The letter was unpopular with many computer hobbyists. So, Gates took measures to ensure that such a situation would not arise again in future by registering his copyright shortly afterwards.

Conclusion

Copyright is an important IP right that no business can ignore in the new economy created by the web.

Given the importance of copyright, businesses in a digital world ought to know enough about the subject in order to appreciate the need to get advice on it when it will impact their plans.

Visit *http://azrights.com/ip-revolution-ch5* to download a copyright assignment

Chapter 6

Why Names Are Important in the Digital World

Copying is so rife in business that if you have a profitable niche or concept, it would be surprising if competitors didn't sooner or later try to capture some of your market share.

They will borrow freely from other businesses that they believe have identified lucrative market opportunities. If they cross the bounds of acceptable, legitimate competition and engage in unethical practices, how will the law help you?

Acceptable copying is where a competitor creates a new business like yours, copying your idea.

People often wish they could stop such copying, and some are disappointed when they learn that writing out their idea and registering it as proof in no way gives them unique rights over their business concept.

Yet, although the name a business chooses for itself or its products can provide powerful protection of the underlying business concept or product, many SMEs either don't really find this protection exciting, or say that the brand isn't that important in their business model because they are likely to be bought out by a business that will not want to use it. Or if they are excited by using a name to protect the underlying concept, they assume they can go and pick whatever name they like and register it as a trade mark in order to have valuable IP.

Scrabulous

Scrabulous was an app created by two Indian brothers that allowed people to play a Scrabble-like game online with friends anywhere in the world. It was a huge hit attracting 600,000 users per day when in 2008, Hasbro, the owner of the Scrabble trade mark, shut them down because their name suggested to the market that this was a similar game to Scrabble. As trade mark law helps to prevent piggy-backing off the success of others' brand, Scrabble was able to get Facebook to pull the Scrabulous app even though it was extremely popular.

The founders had even applied to register a trade mark for their name, clearly unaware of the wide scope of protection that trade marks give. Had they taken advice before using the name, they would have realised the choice was unwise.

The fact that their app had gone viral did not stop Facebook from simply removing it. This paved the way for Zynga to create what is now a highly successful Words with Friends app. The brothers' advantage of being the first to build a Scrabble-like app on Facebook was lost, and we will never know how big Scrabulous would have been today if it had opted for a better name.

Scrabulous is a high profile example of what I see happen all too often. I've known businesses that have spent thousands on a logo and sophisticated website, only to be derailed by a legal issue which could have been avoided had they taken advice.

It's essential to build IP law into the creative process early on. Larger companies are by no means immune to these problems. On the other hand, it happens quite often that one department develops a brand to an advanced stage, and only then does the legal department get involved in the project. It's often too late for the legal team to have much impact, and therefore in-house legal departments have a similar need to raise awareness of IP as IP lawyers have in the world at large. The organisation is the loser, as it wastes money and resources, and either has to rebrand and start again or, more likely, ends up with a far weaker brand than it could have achieved had it taken IP into account sooner.

Names are invariably the primary way in which consumers identify goods and services. A name is the 'sign' that customers use to tell a business apart from its competitors.

What might have previously been regarded as an esoteric specialist subject is now mainstream as a result of the web

IP around names and copyright is the area of law, upon which businesses often need their main advice; to determine whether their business plans are viable, to check out their proposed name, to review contracts for development of software or websites, or for documentation, such as privacy policies and terms of business, which quite often have a social networking element.

Before the widespread adoption of the web, names and trade marks were more the preserve of big household name companies like Proctor and Gamble that had hundreds of product brands. The legal profession was geared around this so that solicitors left it to trade mark attorneys to specialise in names.

Today this demarcation only works for big household names with hundreds or thousands of trade marks to protect. However, it does not serve the interests of SMEs in today's digital economy to have to go to separate firms for names, copyright, contracts and other advice.

Nowadays SMEs are exposed to a global audience in ways that simply did not occur in the industrial era. We have more businesses today than we've ever had before, and because you can market to a global marketplace, it is important to pick names which can help you to stand out, while not infringing on the rights of others. Given the possibility for a business with a good idea to create a substantial niche for itself it is important that the name chosen is one that the business can uniquely own, ideally internationally. It should be a name which creates valuable IP – and that means it must be distinctive and capable of being trade marked.

You should learn to do some essential due diligence checks yourself so you can produce a shortlist of names for further checking by your legal team. It's then important to consider whether to check out the rights to use a name in all territorial areas where you will do business.

I'm not sure why the power of names to protect the underlying concept is not better understood, nor why it is felt not to be important to consult a lawyer when selecting a name.

Should you register your own mark?

A trade mark registration should be planned properly. The correct wording for each classification will take into account current and future plans for the business.

The notion that registering your own trade mark is as good as getting legal help, risks not getting adequate protection.

As mentioned earlier, I've seen SMEs wasting a lot of money filing inappropriate trade marks.

Trade mark

Registering your own mark risks throwing money down the drain, and more seriously, risks that you continue to use an inadequate name. You can register anything if you combine it with a logo. Securing such a registration would give you a false sense of security. It could be that the name you are using can't function as a trade mark so that you're effectively just getting protection for the logo when arguably you don't need such protection at all in the early days. My advice to any ambitious business is to get expert advice on whether the name you're using is legally effective, and suitable for your business, and to use professionals to register what is, likely, your most valuable asset.

Keywords to Google success

One issue that causes confusion when doing business online is that naming gets mixed up with the question of being found online.

The general wisdom among certain online marketing specialists is that you should choose a name (and hence domain brand name) that matches a keyword people will be looking for when seeking your products and services, and by so doing your website will be more easily found by searchers seeking your offerings.

The fact that it might help your website to rise in the search engines is therefore used as reason enough to use a description of your services rather than a name for a business.

This practice has become so widespread that it is now a truism which is not even questioned by those that believe it to be true.

I wonder if this tendency for IP myths to become accepted truths would arise if solicitors as a body were advising their clients on names and other online business issues. I suspect that the trade mark and other considerations have had a lower profile precisely because the

IP profession is so fragmented, with the solicitors profession abdicating responsibility for advising on names to the trade mark profession. This might have been compounded by the fact that few online digital marketing professionals receive any training in IP matters. Yet they regularly help their clients with branding.

This is one reason why we provide brand consultancy services to clients, and support branding agencies to find names by attending name brainstorming sessions where desired.

A brand name is one of the most fundamental aspects of a company's identity. It is too important for any one profession to handle alone. Branding agencies who create the name need to work closely with lawyers who understand IP and trade mark law. It's hard enough to find a good name that is legally available without having inappropriate negativity from a lawyer working on such projects. So, a key consideration for branding agencies when selecting a law firm to work with should be whether the lawyers are commercial and pragmatic enough to realise that there is no such thing as a completely safe name. Naming doesn't happen in a vacuum. The markets in which the client wishes to operate, its products and services, the degree of risk the client is willing to bear, all impact the approach to the naming project, the type of name to opt for, and the price of the due diligence.

The early days of the web

In the early days of the internet, the web was like a small village with perhaps one or two of each type of business: a toy shop, a grocery store, a bookshop, a hotel, and so on. It was therefore common for businesses to call themselves by descriptive names, and to use domain names like toys.com, books.com, pets.com, hotels.com, etc.

As more and more businesses set up on the web, the descriptive, 'small village' approach to naming became more inappropriate but was justified on search engine visibility grounds. Now, despite recent changes to Google's algorithms that reduce the relevance of descriptive keywords, it is still a common view among web professionals that using a descriptive name is the way to go.

Recent changes in Google's algorithm make the benefit of using descriptive names insufficient (if they ever were otherwise) to warrant the loss of distinctiveness that occurs when a business uses a description of its activities instead of a name as its keyword.

There are other ways of being found on the search engines and the sacrifice of using descriptive names is too great to justify abandoning good naming practices.

Even SEOMoz, the online marketing specialist has publically come down in favour of brand names.

An example of the sort of problem that can befall a business with a descriptive name is Hotels.com which was founded in the early days of the web when it was fashionable to use generic descriptive names as a brand name.

Hotels.com

The company applied to register its name as a trade mark, and put forward evidence to persuade the United States Patent and Trademark Office (USPTO) that its brand had acquired distinctiveness during the twenty years it had been in business. (The fact that Hotels.com actually went to this expense is a testament to the importance of trade marks to established businesses.)

After carrying out a nationwide survey of consumers, the company found that consumers regarded Hotels.com as a brand name.

Nevertheless, the USPTO held that the mark was generic, and Hotels.com lost the case.

In opting for a descriptive name, Hotels.com left itself vulnerable. Apart from not being able to trade mark the name, the downside to using a purely descriptive name is that there is little you can do in practical terms to stop a competitor setting up with a similar name and piggy backing off your success. Although on the web there may be only one Hotels.com domain, it does not stop companies calling themselves Hotels com by using other domain names.

People don't necessarily look that closely at the domain name in the browser. Similarly, in the physical world dozens of hotels could call themselves Hotels.com, and divert goodwill away from the original Hotels.com.

Your average customer no longer goes to the effort of entering the whole website url.

We will never know for sure, but I suspect that Hotels. com might have become a far more successful and well-known brand if it had chosen a distinctive name for itself, as Google, Amazon, and countless other online businesses have been savvy enough to do.

The other issue online is that competitors can bid on the name in Adwords. The usual restrictions that apply when you bid on a distinctive brand name do not apply to descriptive names.

Keyword advertising

Google Adwords has become an important tool for many businesses who operate online to attract more customers, advertise locally and globally as well as reach out to the right people.

It is permissible to bid on a competitor's trade mark in order for your ad to appear whenever a searcher is looking for your competitor's brand. This is where a lack of understanding of the intricacies of the law can land you in hot water if you're not given the appropriate advice.

Marks & Spencer and Interflora

In this case Marks & Spencer had been using the Adword 'Interflora' to trigger results for its own flower delivery service. Marks & Spencer, however, is not part of the florist network 'Interflora' and so the question was whether using Interflora's name in Adwords amounted to trade mark infringement. While bidding on a competitor's trade mark does not in itself constitute trade mark infringement, if the ad as a whole suggests a connection with the original trade mark owner, there are strong grounds for arguing that it infringes.

The litigation between Marks and Spencer and Interflora which ensued is still ongoing. The Court of Appeal recently decided to retry the dispute. The High Court had ruled that M&S had infringed Interflora's trade mark by bidding on the word 'Interflora', but the Court of Appeal doubted that a significant proportion of consumers would mistakenly believe that M&S was part of Interflora's network.

In considering whether the ad as a whole suggests a connection with a trade mark owner, the issue is whether the so-called 'reasonably well-informed and reasonably attentive Internet user' would be confused into believing that the ad emanates from the trade mark proprietor (in this case Interflora)?

In the High Court decision in the M&S case in May 2013, the court thought that a significant proportion of consumers who searched for 'Interflora', and then clicked on M&S's ads, believed that M&S's flower delivery service was part of the Interflora network.

> The decision of the Court of Appeal underlines the difficulty of determining whether or not bidding on a competitor's keyword infringes their trade mark. The answer depends on the facts of each case. Relevant factors are what the ad says, what page it leads to and the relationship between the parties.

Also crucial in practical terms is whether the trade mark owner on whose keywords you are bidding has the resources to sue you.

The key message is that it is not risk-free. Litigation is possible and may deter some people from bidding on competitors' keywords.

The point to note here though, is that it is difficult to stop competitors using the same or similar names in keyword rich domain names or descriptive names, as they do not have the same protection as is afforded to a distinctive name like Interflora. This underlines yet again the importance of choosing legally effective names in a digital environment.

Descriptive names are a poor choice

I want to end this section by stressing that choosing a descriptive name is setting yourself up for many problems down the line. A name that says on the tin what the business does is not a name. It can't function as a trade mark. You don't create as valuable a business as a result. You create valuable assets by associating the innovation that drives your business with something that is simple and memorable. Think Apple.

Choosing a descriptive name is analogous to leaving your house unlocked because it makes you more vulnerable to competitors stealing your market share. A descriptive name is like using a bucket with holes in it because you lose some of the IP value that would otherwise accrue uniquely to your business.

These days, as with any brand name, distinctive names work much more effectively on the web. The descriptive-named businesses of the early web days came and went. Despite enjoying serious venture capital backing, they have faded into oblivion. All they have left behind are valuable domain names that may have changed hands several times by now, and are principally valuable for search purposes. For example, books. com redirects to Barnes & Noble, bringing extra traffic to that site.

Poor advice on naming

If names are chosen without involving a trade mark expert, the business potentially loses out. If you are not armed with the knowledge to give informed consent when an inadequate name is developed for you, it means the absence of legal input before finalising the decision effectively deprives you of knowing the wider considerations that you should take into account.

So all branding agencies should find IP lawyers to collaborate with when choosing names for their clients to ensure the names they choose are capable of functioning as trade marks.

What not to do

A cautionary tale based on a real life case

An entrepreneur had spent over £100,000 building a website and optimising the site for search and social media when its domain names were confiscated. It was using a domain name very similar to the market leader in its industry. This wasn't a well-known name like Apple that anyone could have told him might be a problem. The name meant nothing to people outside his industry, and he had chosen the name himself.

So when the business lost its domains, it lost all the money it had poured into optimising the website, and there was no-one to blame for the disaster. The business never recovered from this set back and closed down soon after.

The moral of the story is that anyone helping a business, in this case web developers, should suggest to them that they get their domain name checked out with an IP lawyer. The more knowledgeable that industries which create IP for SMEs become about IP, the more they can help their clients to reach for success and avoid disasters.

When looking for suitable digital IP lawyers, check whether they understand search engine optimisation so they can hold their own when discussing with web or branding agencies why alternatives to descriptive names should be pursued. The web is changing fast so that basing your naming decisions on the latest approach to SEO is short sighted. What may have been the accepted way to name a business when the internet first started is no longer valid today.

Social media is adding to the pace of change. The need to stand out from the competition is more important than ever in the crowded web landscape, and that calls for a distinctive name.

Some businesses only appreciate the inability of their name to protect them against unfair competition once they've attracted copycats. When they find they have few remedies available to them, it is often too late to change names. Rebranding costs a lot of time and money, and results in loss of the recognition your business has already obtained.

Conclusion

Given that businesses market to a global audience when they sell online, it is essential when they're choosing names for their ecommerce site that they are well informed.

While descriptive names are effective from a marketing point of view because they inform consumers what the business does, they are inadequate to protect the underlying business concept, and for preventing competitors from piggy-backing off your success.

Visit *http://azrights.com/ip-revolution-ch6* to find out more about the do's and don'ts of naming.

Chapter 7

Other IPRs in a Digital Age

Apart from copyright and trade marks, there are other important IP issues to address in the digital world. Confidentiality is a most fundamental aspect of IP to understand in the new economy, especially as Big Data is so important to every industry.

Keeping information secret is the way to manage IP risks, although this sits uncomfortably with the open nature of the web, and new approaches to marketing which the web enables.

Online success is often about spreading your ideas and being known for a particular niche. So, people can get the wrong impression about IP as being all about keeping everything secret and the very opposite of disseminating your ideas freely, but of course, it is not at all necessary to keep everything close to your chest. You just need to be canny about what information you publicise, and what you keep private.

Crowd-funding is an increasingly popular way for businesses to raise funds so if you are going to raise funds in this way it is important to know when secrecy might be more prudent than openness.

Crowd-funding

Crowd-funding sites such as KickStarter, have grown in popularity. The concept is simple – you have an idea, formulate the logistics of the plan, and then upload the idea to a crowd-funding website, where millions of potential investors can scrutinise it, and if they like it, pledge to invest in the project. If the project raises the target capital, the funds are automatically transferred, and the idea becomes a reality. If the target is not met, no money is transferred, so no investors lose out.

Essentially it's *Dragons' Den* for the web generation, leveraging the almost perfect liquidity of the online marketplace.

While this might be a viable option for certain business ideas, there will be others which should stay away from crowd-funding platforms in their early stages. For example, a product-based concept such as Mandy Haberman's Anywayup Cup could not have succeeded had she not patented the cup before going to market. As it was, she had to fend off copycat products through litigation in the courts. Without a patent, it would have been impossible to compete against well-resourced manufacturers.

In their haste to rush to market quickly, many entrepreneurs are making a classic mistake – failing to protect their intellectual property (IP) before revealing their ideas. Patents are only granted if an invention is novel, and has not been disclosed to third parties. Therefore, if you raise investment through crowd-funding sites, before securing a patent, then you lose the possibility of patenting the concept later on.

Many entrepreneurs fail to seek legal advice before trying to raise funds through crowd-funding sites. They naively assume these sites must have thought through the legal aspects on their behalf.

However, in practice you need to find the funds to file an initial patent pending application, whether you're speaking to angel investors or seeking crowd-funding because few investors agree to sign non-disclosure agreements (NDAs) before listening to your opening pitch. Your credibility is bolstered enormously if you understand this, and have taken steps to protect your concept beforehand. They will deem you more attractive.

Another issue is whether you are infringing on the rights of others. Formlabs, a team of PhD students, managed to raise just under $3m (£2m) to commercialise an accessible 3D printer. But the virtual high fives soon turned sour as an established company, 3D Systems, sued them for patent infringement.

Another issue to be aware of is that well-resourced competitors are scouring these sites, and are free to exploit the technology or concept you just shared with the world. Would you be sabotaging your idea by alerting someone to it who is well placed to copy it?

In 2010, Scott Wilson was congratulated for successfully raising $942,578 on KickStarter to launch the TikTok Lunatik watch kit, a sleek new aluminium watch strap, which converted an iPod Nano into a touchscreen watch.

The design and trade mark had not been protected. It proved immensely popular. Copycat imitations began to spring up around the web. The market is now flooded with fake Lunatik watches.

The moral is clear. If you're considering using a crowd-funding platform, make sure you understand the IP implications before doing so.

In a digital environment where information is freely sharable, think carefully about the information you share with others online. By understanding IP principles and the business environment it is more possible to work out when secrecy is appropriate.

When it comes to patentability, disclosure of ideas outside the context of a confidential relationship will jeopardise the chances of securing a patent, so in open innovation projects it is vital to have confidentiality agreements in place between companies collaborating on research and development projects, to preserve the possibility of patenting any innovations that may emerge from the collaboration.

Apple's iPhone

Steve Jobs gave a presentation of the iPhone in 2007 which was captured on video and during it he even said 'boy have we patented it!' However, they hadn't patented it in Germany until after that presentation. Then, six years later, when Apple wanted to rely on the patent, that video was enough evidence to invalidate the German patent for one of the iPhone features.

The basic premise of patents is that you explain to the public your new technology and in return receive certain monopoly rights for a period of time, provided you continue to pay the necessary fees. If you want to avoid disclosing your innovation, and can effectively keep it a secret and still exploit it, patenting may not be for you.

Do bear in mind, though, that someone else might devise the same invention themselves independently, and if you don't have a patent, you will not be able to stop them getting a patent.

Trade secrets are an alternative to patenting.

Coca-Cola

Coca-Cola is a good example of a company that has used trade secrecy as a way of keeping its cola recipe a secret for more than 100 years. Reportedly, at any one time only three people within the Coca-Cola organisation worldwide have access to the secret formula.

That is the point about secret recipes and know how. If you don't protect them well and the information gets out into the public domain, you have lost your valuable IP. So, any IP that depends on confidentiality needs careful consideration in terms of the practical measures as well as the legal terms you might use to protect it.

Any ideas you have for a new business concept, trade secrets you might want to divulge to others (such as know-how in relation to patented subject matter you might be licensing, know how to which your employees have access) all are well worth discussing with an IP lawyer before divulging them to others. Even deciding whether to disclose information under a non-disclosure agreement should be carefully considered. It's only once you understand the limitations of NDAs in terms of protecting your information, that it would be appropriate to proceed to discuss your ideas with third parties such as web designers.

Patents

For many businesses patents may never be relevant or may be a one off matter. However, given that patents are a form of IP which you need to register to secure, it pays to have some general knowledge as to how to keep your ideas secret. You are then better placed to secure rights to an invention if you ever wish to do so.

For some businesses patent protection is critical to success. For example, if you have an innovative business idea for a product, such as Mandy Hauberman had for her Anywayup Cup innovation, a larger, well-resourced manufacturer would present a threat if you had no patent protection. They could simply enter the market and use their greater financial muscle to take over your share of the market.

A good way to understand the difference between design protection and patents is that the visual features of something like the Dyson vacuum cleaner will be protected by design registration, while the way it functions without a bag is something that is protected by patents.

Mandy Haberman

The inventor of the Anywayup Cup was soon copied when manufacturers realised there was consumer interest in her product. They produced similar cups, and she took them to court to protect her business. She has said:

'Because I had patents I was able to go to court, defend my idea, enforce my patent rights and that meant that I kept my monopoly in the market. This made me a lot of money; if I had not had the patents, I would not have made anything.'

So, if you want to make it big, avoid embarking on projects where patent protection is essential to your business model until you have the resources to file an initial patent application.

These are the types of business in which the dragons in *Dragons' Den* lose interest when they discover there is no IP protection, or that the patent protection is too weak.

Owning IP puts you in a strong position

Don't let reservations about whether you can afford to enforce your IP rights, stop you protecting your rights in the first place. Often, simply owning IP rights is enough to avoid disputes arising. Not securing your IP is more, rather than less, likely to result in litigation for your business. Litigation is extremely expensive, particularly litigation over patents.

Business process patents

While patents offer an important incentive to innovation, and a just reward to those who develop new technology, which benefits society, the trend in recent litigation in the USA has been to avoid setting the bar for patent protection too low.

Every non-trivial piece of software involves a series of technical problems overcome through the innovative application of a developer's expertise and experience. Code is written and problems are overcome daily by software engineers worldwide. The 1-Click 'innovation' by Amazon was far from the most complex of these and for many years Amazon was able to stop competitors providing a 1-Click checkout functionality on their websites simply because of Amazon's patent, which was subsequently nullified.

The current approach to software patents

The US's current less lenient approach to software patents has meant that Amazon's 1-click patent has been invalidated.

There is still, nevertheless, a difference in how the UK patent system approaches software patents when compared to the US and European Patent Office. On the whole the UK is the most restrictive of the three in its approach to patenting.

The fear is that smaller players in the software field who cannot afford to acquire patent portfolios of software or to pay for licensing agreements, may be forced out of the market altogether.

Patents, particularly software-based ones, are potentially rife with infringement litigation, especially within the US. This can make it particularly difficult for a small company to decide whether to spend what might be a huge proportion of its IP budget on patent protection. Certain companies hold portfolios of patents with the pure objective of enforcing their rights against purported infringers, and sometimes even against non-copiers.

Enforcement of patents is their business rather than manufacturing or research, and the objective is to collect royalty income from their portfolios.

Tech and social media companies commonly fear that patents might put an end to their business if used against them.

Alternatively, they might look to buy their competitors' IP in order to create the market conditions favourable to them. For example, Facebook purchased WhatsApp for an eye watering $22 billion not because of its technology but simply because WhatsApp has an exponentially growing user base.

This serves to illustrate the value of IP no matter how simple or complex your idea.

Design protection

The way things look is often the reason why you buy them, be it a pair of shoes, watch, necklace or other item. That is why you should protect the visual differentiators of your business.

In a digital world, the importance of registering the shape of unique designs increases because it is so easy for competitors to have sight of your new designs and copy them.

The iPod, many perfume bottles, fashion garments like handbags, pieces of furniture such as chairs or coffee tables, or packaging like a plastic bottle for washing liquid, are all examples of designs that are capable of being registered. By registering, you 'own' the visual aspects of your unique designs, and strengthen your rights in them.

Rights secured through registration or contracts

Given the global nature of business in a digital environment, it's necessary for small businesses to protect their IP strategically, which might include protecting it in key countries worldwide.

The law of the country in which you live is the starting point for securing initial rights, and determining the additional benefits you can secure through further registrations or appropriate use of a contract.

Although IP is often associated with registration of trade marks, designs or patents, contracts play an extremely important part in securing your IP too. For example, if you jointly develop something with someone else that you could patent, it is going to be your contract as much as patent law that determines the scope of your rights. So it is crucial to consider all IP rights when protecting a business, and not to just focus on patents.

If your business has an online platform, the terms on which you grant people access to your website also present an opportunity to enhance your protection through contractual agreement.

Conclusion

The number of IP rights is expanding all the time due to the rapid development of technologies. This means new IP systems have arisen to protect existing or new subject matter (for example, plant variety protection and circuit layouts). The protection of semiconductors, and database rights are other examples of how IP rights are having to expand in the light of digitisation and the development of new technologies.

Unless the law finds ways to protect the investment that companies put into creating new things, business people would have little incentive to do so. So the tension caused by the ease with which copyright content can be copied in a digital world has been a challenge to the law, and continues to be. In addition we now have 3D printing which is the next challenge for IP law.

Visit *http://azrights.com/ip-revolution-ch7* to download an article on 3D printing which raises many IP issues.

Part Three

IP Practicalities

Chapter 8

Practical Application of IP – Franchising and Licensing

A key reason why IP issues matter so much to any business is that ownership, control and use of individual IP elements can be shared with different parties in exchange for royalties.

Licensing is an important way in which to scale a business and increase its revenues. For example, the Virgin group makes about £120m a year purely from licensing its brand to other companies.

The Virgin brand has been valued at roughly £1bn, and is a useful case study for anyone hoping to grow their business through licensing and franchising.

If you own property which you rent out, you can earn an income from it for the duration of the lease. However, you are limited to one tenancy arrangement because it is physical property. To enjoy it, the tenant will want to occupy it, and will not want to share use of it with others; there is a natural limit to the income that a landlord can obtain from one property.

The difference when you have intangible property, such as copyright in a piece of software, or trade mark in a brand name, is that there is no physical limit to the number of people who can be given a right to use your property. As such the revenues you can earn from intellectual property far exceed those you can earn from physical property.

At the heart of licensing and franchising is ownership of intellectual property rights.

Assuming you own a range of IP rights, you have an option of whether to license your business format as a whole or to licence just some aspects of your IP.

To some extent, whether you will use licensing or franchising depends on what it is you have in your business. It is not always easy to distinguish between the two. In fact, some 'licensing' deals are so close to franchising that they blur the boundary between the two.

The distinction matters because franchising involves more formalities and cost to set up. Licensing, on the other hand, is less prescriptive as it covers many possible business arrangements. It enables you to make income from all kinds of intellectual property – your know-how, creative output, reputation, patents, trade marks, designs, and so on.

It is possible to license as much or as little of your business as you like. However, when doing so, you want to make sure you have the correct IP strategy in place.

As successful as the Virgin franchise is, when Virgin first floated in 1986 it was subject to a lot of scrutiny from analysts. The increased publicity which came with being a public company revealed that many of Virgin's ventures were ailing, and consequently cost the Virgin brand its market confidence.

Branson delisted it in 1988, sold 25 percent of his music group and restructured many of his companies. Although a small detail in the history of its media empire, the important message here is that if you intend to franchise your brand you should understand that placing your trade mark on anything will not necessarily guarantee that the franchise will be profitable, no matter how important, big or well-known you are.

An IP strategy is crucial to understanding your most important IP assets and how they might apply in different sectors and countries. When licensing and franchising, it is crucial to ensuring the growth of your company.

To understand the difference between licensing and franchising, the starting point is to look at what each term means.

Franchising

Franchising is a way to scale a business, once it is successful and proven. It involves finding franchisees with the skills necessary to operate branches of the same business.

McDonald's is one of the best known examples of a business that has grown through franchising. (By contrast, Starbucks has grown by opening its own branches).

Clearly, the investment involved to grow a business through franchising will be much lower than that required to grow it by opening your own branches in other parts of the city, country and world.

Franchising involves a cost to set up, but once you've got the franchise in place, the costs of extending the business to other areas is much lower. Indeed you'd expect to be paid a fee by the franchisee in order to buy the rights to operate the franchise, and ongoing royalties on the income they generate.

You can franchise almost any type of business. Under a franchise arrangement, the owner (franchisor) retains control of the brand and licenses (that is, grants permissions to) the franchisee to use its successful business model and brand. In exchange, the franchisee puts up the initial capital for the business, helps to promote the brand and pays a licence fee. The franchisor supports its franchisees by providing training, know-how, marketing and other resources and skills.

Licensing of intellectual property (IP) is at the heart of a franchise contract. So, in fact, a franchise includes licensing. Typically, this will cover know how and other confidential information, trade marks, logos and designs, and copyright materials. For some businesses there may be patents, too.

An essential element of a franchise (and one of the features that distinguishes it from a straight licence) relates to the formalities involved in setting up a franchise, and the degree of control the franchisor retains.

A franchise agreement will usually give the franchisor the ability to control how the business is run. For example, if a customer visits a branch of McDonald's while on a trip abroad, expecting the familiar service they are used to at home, it is important that they should not be disappointed. Any unpleasant surprises due to changes in the business format could damage McDonald's brand generally, not just that particular outlet. For that reason, the franchise agreement must contain strict quality control provisions.

Licensing

The essence of licensing (which is also the basis of franchising) is that the owner retains ownership of the IP while granting others the right to use it. The terms can vary considerably.

Having said that, some licensing can look a lot like franchising. For example, in the 1850s the inventor of the sewing machine, Isaac Singer, sold licences to entrepreneurs to sell his machines in different parts of the USA. He also offered training in the use of the machines. In this case, the IP licensed was a patent in the sewing machines, the Singer brand name, and know how to operate the machines. Strictly, this was licensing, but it is so similar to what we think of as franchising today that some people even consider Singer to be the father of franchising.

At the other end of the spectrum, imagine a car wash that has developed a successful process for getting its customers to opt for hot wax and other optional extras. The car wash might license that process to other car wash businesses in return for royalties. These other companies might make payments each month in return for the right to use the original car wash's way of promoting the wax, so that more customers buy it. In this example, the IP being licensed is pure 'know how'. Generally, know how alone is difficult to protect, particularly internationally. Usually, it will be part of a bundle of other IP rights, in which case it is easier to enforce and protect.

Another example of licensing is a software licence, such as for Microsoft Office. The software is licensed to you – you do not own anything more than the right to use it, subject to the terms and conditions of the licence.

There are many choices to make when setting up new licence arrangements. Microsoft happens to have set up its licences in the ways they are structured, namely one licence per user.

Another software business could opt to do things differently, for example, instead of granting access to a particular user, they could grant multiple users access to the software subject to an organizational maximum number of users at any one time. Such a licence might more closely match the needs of a world where organisations employ part time and casual staff, and would be able to manage their overall usage without having to invest in a separate licence for each named user.

Just a small difference like this could have a huge impact on a business' success in a market where there are several competitors targeting businesses for market share. So, never assume that the terms on which you provide your intellectual property are just small print to address as an afterthought. On the contrary; your terms of business are at the heart of your business.

Brand licensing

If you have built up a brand name, one way to scale your business is to issue a licence to a third party to deliver a related product under your brand name. So, a successful fashion designer might license a perfume manufacturer to create a perfume range for its label.

Another option if you have a successful product or brand, is to grant a licence to someone to sell your product under their own brand name. An example is the model Twiggy producing a range of clothes for Marks & Spencer.

Similarly, a cook such as Nigella Lawson can and does grant a licence to others to sell cooking utensils and crockery using her name on their products. Nigella derives substantial royalties from this type of licensing activity.

On the other hand, failing to obtain a licence can be a fatal error. An example is the infamous Rihanna case. Here, the high-street clothing megastore Topshop had used an image of Rihanna on one of the t-shirts it was selling without first obtaining a licence or permission from Rihanna. The celebrity was able to sue Topshop for £3.3 million in a passing off action.

Disney Licence

Disney is such an established licensing model that they have set up a page letting potential licensees know how to apply for a licence to use their characters and brand on third party merchandise. The page in question reads as follows:

'A Disney licence can give your product instant recognition, marketability and desirability. In addition, products featuring licenced characters can sell for more money than generic competing products. Of course, all of that comes at a price. Obtaining a Disney licence can be time-consuming and expensive, but having a proven track record in your field and cash on hand to pay up-front expenses and royalties will increase your odds of getting one'.

Luxury brands are highly sought after for licensing, as their brand brings a cachet to the product, to which they lend their name. But brands should beware of veering too far away from their market or offering licences too liberally.

Pierre Cardin

Pierre Cardin is an example of a brand that has devalued its name by engaging in indiscriminate licensing.

It reportedly has 400 licensees worldwide, many relating to products far removed from fashion. He started by licensing his name for porcelain crockery in 1968. Now there are Cardin toilets, strollers and heating units, and numerous other products.

While twenty years ago, fashion labels began to realise that too much licensing harmed their global reputation, and began to carefully handpick their licenses in areas that are related to the core business, Pierre Cardin continued to farm out his name to thousands of products worldwide.

As a result, the Pierre Cardin brand has lost much of its cachet.

Brand extensions that involve licensing your products or services to different categories are more likely to fail.

For instance, Harley Davidson perfume proved to be an extension too far. And despite the fact that Virgin has been able to apply its brand to records, financial services, airlines and a variety of other products and services, it failed in its bid to extend its brand to cola.

However, one company that has managed to pull off this feat is the EasyJet group. The 'Easy' prefix is now associated with a variety of different products and services, easyCar; easyHotel; easyBus; easyVan; easyOffice; easyPizza; easyGym; easyProperty; easyFoodstore; easyMoney.

You are more likely to succeed in extending your brand to areas which are not commonly sought after. Your well-known name can generate value this way when you are not competing with well-established megabrands.

Potential of licensing and franchising

IP rights lie at the foundation of licensing and franchising. Although in the early days of a business there may be nothing worthy of licensing or franchising, these ways of scaling a business should be borne in mind when creating the foundations.

By carefully creating and managing IP, and ensuring that the business secures ownership in the IP it generates, you can ensure your business is well placed to license or franchise its format should it succeed. Keeping knowhow under wraps will also be an element of managing IP.

Then once there is something that others might want to licence it will be straightforward to scale the business. Unfortunately, businesses that leave IP issues until they are poised for growth, such as to launch their franchises, can find at the eleventh hour that they don't have the rights to use the name they've been using, or they don't own the copyright to some important element in their business, like their logo or software. These are just some reasons for attending to IP issues at an early stage.

As franchising is expensive to set up, licensing can be a good way to start if you are interested in franchising your business. Rather than diving straight into franchising with all the due diligence and formalities that it entails, you could start by finding a few licensees who are willing to license some or all of your business model. (Although beware that in some countries, such as the USA, and certain parts of the EU where franchising is heavily regulated, you want to avoid calling what is essentially a franchise a licence. It is unlikely to escape the regulators' attention. They will look to the essence of the agreement rather than its name).

A worthy note of warning, however: if you intend to license your products and/or services, including your trade mark or trade name outside the EU, you will not benefit from the protection of harmonised EU trade mark laws. The consequence is that without including the appropriate legal provisions there is little you can do if that licensee goes to register your trade mark. It is a common occurrence and it would also mean that it would not even be possible to oppose the application. You might find yourself in a position of trying to buy it back at an extortionate rate which is not desirable when you are starting out on your franchise.

Conclusion

Whether you are licensing or franchising, the important thing is to have solid IP underpinning your business, covering the territories in which you are intending to grant licences.

Your brand, patents, knowhow, trade marks etc., are precious assets, which should be properly protected, and the terms on which you grant licences or franchises need to be carefully considered in consultation with your intellectual property lawyer.

Visit *http://azrights.com/ip-revolution-ch8* to download a franchise agreement and understand the range of decisions to be made.

Chapter 9

Why it's Possible to Ignore IP

If IP is that important, why do so many businesses get away with virtually ignoring the subject in their early years?

I suspect if a study were undertaken of the many businesses that fail every year, we would find a number were due to not taking an important IP issue on board.

A common IP mistake concerns the choice of name. It's important to understand that the reason a name issue may not cause problems for a business is that many of them start out with names which they later change once their concept is proven. They might have been temporarily infringing on someone else's brand, or using an otherwise inadequate name. However, they never experience an adverse consequence in doing so because they are 'saved' by their decision to rebrand.

Alternatively, their business never reaches sufficient success levels to threaten an existing trade mark owner.

Many others are not so lucky.

No sooner do some businesses start than they receive notice that they are infringing on someone's brand. This can have serious consequences for those that have invested significantly in their branding, or who simply don't have the time and resources to overcome such a setback.

It's easy to fall foul of someone else's trade mark rights when you set up or change your business in any way. Extending into new areas and even narrowing your focus in an area could result in your infringing on someone else's trade mark rights. It's also dangerous to imitate a well-known brand, and the below case is a good example of the commercial power of a well-known trade mark:

L'Oréal v Bellure

In this case, the famous perfume manufacturer L'Oréal successfully sued a much smaller company that sold perfumes which were not intended to compete with the up-market brand. Rather they were cheaper 'smell-alike' alternatives to the real thing for a less wealthy demographic who would generally not be able to afford the price of expensive perfumes. The smell-alike perfumes were held to be infringing because they were advertised on comparison lists against several of L'Oréal's brands. Further, it was said that the imitation of the bottles and packaging were also infringing on the reputation of L'Oréal's trade marks. The cheaper products did not bear L'Oréal's trade marks and nor did anyone think any less of L'Oréal's perfumes. However, the court found that the smaller company had taken unfair advantage of L'Oreal's allure.

An important point to bear in mind is how you market your products. If you're lucky, a trade mark owner with better rights will find out about you straight away. Rebranding is hugely disruptive, and adversely impacts the business because you effectively suddenly vanish. You are unlikely to be able to redirect your website to your new name. You will also have to change your marketing materials, get a new logo, business cards, and start over with a completely new name. It's a huge distraction.

The later the trade mark owner approaches you to rebrand, the more devastating the consequences will be for you. Running a business without doing thorough trade mark searches (and while you're at it, claiming the name by registering it as a trade mark) is running a risk that could literally wipe you out at some point in the future when the business might be very successful, and a source of income for you.

Although not as a result of legal proceedings, the Symantec rebrand illustrates how difficult it can be to establish yourself with a new name.

Symantec

Symantec, the technology company that provides security software, has reportedly spent $1.28 billion in its rebranding of VeriSign authentication technology, to Symantec. The Symantec rebrand is part of a global rebranding of all of its products which has seen a huge slump in share price.

The case illustrates how rebranding is not only expensive in the most extreme cases, but also it can put you at a significant disadvantage because consumers will lose the association and loyalty to the brand and your presence in the market place will falter.

So, for the unlucky ones, their infringement of someone else's trade mark rights, or lack of adequate IP protection goes undetected for many years. Neglect in the early years can and does leave them considerably exposed. However, we don't often hear about the misfortunes of small businesses that go under due to some IP flaw because it's simply not newsworthy, nor do legal issues get litigated in the courts. So, necessarily there is a dearth of case studies involving small business.

By looking at the big household name brands, we find plenty of examples of IP problems. If these substantial businesses encounter issues, they can afford to put up a fight. So we can extrapolate from their stories by considering what a lesser business might do if it hit similar problems. In other words, the successful resolution of a problem for a big brand often simply comes down to their having enough money to appeal a decision, or negotiate a solution, or to rebrand. Would an SME have the resources to achieve a similar resolution if disaster struck? And remember that disaster is much more likely to strike for SMEs because many of them will not have had access to legal help to prevent disasters, whereas for household names it's when something slips through their legal safety net that problems tend to arise.

It is also important to understand some of the subtleties of IP law to appreciate why there does not need to be a dramatic consequence to ignoring IP, for there to nevertheless be a severe impact on a business which limits its potential. So, the owners may never be aware of the loss for the business.

For example, you might find yourself like Daisuke Inoue, the Japanese businessman, who invented the karaoke machine. He hadn't patented the invention, and others made significant sums of money from the invention while he made nothing. You would be aware if you could have patented something like Karaoke, and would have some idea of what you lost.

Alternatively, you could be like László József Bíró, a Hungarian born inventor, who in 1938 had patented the universally known ballpoint pen, or biro for short. Before he had the chance to benefit from its huge commercial potential, László Bíró decided to sell the patent to Marcel Bic for $2million, around £11.6 million today. Bic soon used it as the main product of his Bic Company which is now reported to sell an estimated 15 million pens every day, and over 100 billion ballpoint pens globally. That is enough to draw a line to the moon and back more than 320,000 times, and to make £11.6 million look like short change.

On the other hand, you may never know what you could have had exclusive right over, and hence earned more revenues from. What you don't know you lost is not going to worry you. Although it should. Most people are in business to, among other things, make money. So, why wouldn't you want to maximise your revenues by taking account of IP?

In other cases, it may be that you could have had a more successful business had you known how to protect your distinctive branding.

For example, Coca-Cola knew how to protect its branding, which is why it was able to secure exclusive rights over its distinctive bottle shape.

To get a monopoly right over something like the iconic Coca Cola bottle shape involves planning early and taking a long term approach.

Coca-Cola

Coca-Cola was able to trade mark its bottle shape having used a design registration early on, and stopped anyone else making such a bottle for some 14 years. During this period, Coca-Cola used its large advertising budget to associate the bottle shape in the public's mind with Coca Cola. Towards the end of the design registration's life, Coca-Cola was able to trade mark the bottle shape. This was only possible because Coca-Cola could show that when people saw the bottle shape on its own they equated it with goods originating from Coca-Cola. In other words, the bottle shape had become an identifier.

Now that Coca-Cola has a trade mark, it has a permanent, exclusive right over this distinctive bottle shape. Provided it renews its trade mark and continues to use the bottle shape, nobody else may ever use the same bottle shape. This is powerful IP indeed.

Coca-Cola is a very good example of a company that has used IP laws to good effect to create a very strong brand.

The purpose of a good name goes beyond brand building

You may never be aware that you could have had a more successful business had you taken account of the IP in your name.

The owners of the business Airbnb would have had much less success if they had given their business a descriptive name like Bed and Breakfast in Host Home Abroad. They would have struggled to stand out from the various copycat businesses that sprung up once their good idea was out there for all to know and copy.

Copying is inevitable. But if you don't stand out in a recognisable way, how can people find your business? To tell each other about your brand they need to readily identify and find you. With descriptive names it is not possible to stop competitors calling themselves by misleadingly similar names. You can't uniquely own a descriptive name.

I am sometimes approached by businesses which started out using a descriptive name for their new innovative website concept. They invariably want to stop a competitor who has spotted the business opportunity and entered the market with a better website, using a similar descriptive name. My advice to rebrand and use a distinctive name, turning the former name into a tag line often falls on deaf ears. Yet the best way to fight off competitors using similar descriptive names is to have a distinctive name. If you, the original business, don't want to be one of many generic named businesses offering that concept, you have to stand out from the crowd, and the way to do that, apart from being the best, is to have a distinctive name. It's a losing battle otherwise, and it may be too late anyway to become uniquely associated with the concept by adopting a distinctive name once you've already started out with a descriptive name

The success of the Zumba business is largely down to its IP strategy, specifically around its name.

Zumba

Founders Alberto 'Beto' Perez, Alberto Perlman and Alberto Aghion created a dance fitness programme that quickly became a worldwide success. Zumba involves elements of dance and aerobics, with choreography incorporating styles ranging from hip-hop to samba and martial arts.

Zumba Fitness is the organisation responsible for selling and distributing Zumba videos and products. It is estimated that approximately 14 million people take weekly Zumba classes in over 140,000 locations across more than 185 countries.

If a similar company was starting out and focused primarily on how to protect its copyright in the choreography of the dance to prevent competitors copying its dance routine, it would be barking up the wrong tree. The IP asset with most potential value in such a business model is the name rather than copyright in the dance itself.

Copying of a dance routine is difficult to prove, and is less likely to threaten the business than copying its name. The public will associate a dance with the name Zumba, even though they may not be sufficiently familiar with the dance routine itself to actually recognise it as a Zumba dance, unless someone refers to it by that name.

However, not any random name will do. It is worth thinking about your name carefully, given that it is what you will be using to answer the phone, to promote and advertise your business. It's also what your customers will use to recommend your product or service.

This quote, from Oscar Wilde's *The Importance of Being Earnest*, demonstrates just how much faith can be placed in a name alone.

> *'It had always been a girlish dream of mine to love someone whose name was Ernest. There is something in that name that seems to inspire absolute confidence.'*

Undoubtedly, a name can evoke certain reactions and emotional responses. It can give customers an idea or feeling about your business from the outset, before they have even experienced working with you. Therefore, choosing a name for your brand is an important task that should not be taken lightly.

Pick a name that suits what your product or service is trying to do. For example, Azrights is a made-up name derived from 'AZ of Rights'. The name was chosen to indicate that we provide a one-stop-shop – that is the A to Z of IP rights services. One of the problems I had spotted in the market was the sheer complexity for SMEs to know which type of IP service provider to consult. So providing all the main services in one place is what the name is designed to evoke.

When choosing a name, think about what is unique about the brand you are trying to create. Who is your target audience? How do you want to make people feel?

Having an arbitrary name like 'Zumba' means that you will need to set aside a sufficient budget to market your name, to associate the brand values to that service and/or product. The more random the name the more marketing is required.

The reason why descriptive names are used is that it is easier to alert consumers as to what you're selling which makes it more convenient to find you. However, it also means that your company cannot distinguish itself from others.

It is quite common for SMEs embarking on new businesses to consult us because they are primarily motivated by IP that will present a barrier to entry into their space and stop competitors engaging in a similar line of business. Patent and copyright protection to prevent copying of the business format, therefore, have strong appeal. So much so that some entrepreneurs lose interest in pursuing IP protection for their ideas simply because they are not able to get a patent to stop competitors copying them. They do not appreciate the power of other IP, such as trade marks, to attract customers and prevent unfair competition.

So while it's true that for some business models you should not proceed without patent protection, it is a fundamental mistake to assume that patents are the best form of IP for every business idea.

The business model will dictate your most important IP asset and protection. Often all the various IP rights, including your terms of business, combine together to provide very effective overall IP protection.

Trade marks are the way the law protects a business against various competitive practices that inevitably arise for a business when it succeeds. You don't need to be aiming to be a brand, for trade marks to be relevant to you. Even if the aim is to create a successful business to sell to a buyer who may not use the same name, it is vital for your business to have a good protectable brand name in the meantime.

Microsoft Windows

Microsoft's delay in applying to register the name of its Windows operating system nearly lost it the chance to secure a registration. Although Microsoft first introduced its Windows software in 1985, it did not file a trade mark application until 1990. By then Windows was so well known that the US Patent and

Trademark Office (USPTO) initially rejected Microsoft's trade mark application on the grounds that the Windows mark was 'merely descriptive' in relation to computer software.

By 1990, many people associated the Windows interface with the way in which the software displayed the user's desktop. Microsoft kept arguing its case, and fought hard to secure a registration. Eventually, in 1995 the USPTO granted the Windows trade mark application. In the meantime, Microsoft had continued to gain market share for its Windows software, and it would have been a huge blow to its marketing plans if the trade mark had not been granted.

Following that error with the Windows trade mark, Microsoft made yet another error recently when it used the Skydrive name, only to have to rebrand to Onedrive when Sky objected to it. This goes to show that even the largest corporations are not immune to the potentially crippling effects of mismanaged IP rights.

A small business with such problems would not have had the resources to persevere until its mark was granted, and to rebrand after establishing its product under a particular name.

SMEs probably experience even more problems than high profile brands that litigate or come to the attention of the newspapers because they will often lack the resources to prevent problems. Bigger brands are generally well advised, and it's only occasionally, when something slips through the net (so that the branding department fails to liaise with the legal department), that they encounter the sort of high profile problems reported in the media.

I suspect IP disasters are proving costly for many businesses. The consequences for SMEs can be grave and could even stop a company dead in its tracks. A lack of awareness is no longer a valid excuse.

Consumer electronics giant Apple is one such example.

Apple

Apple, the world's most valuable company, found itself having to pay $60million in a settlement to Proview International Holdings regarding the iPad trade mark in China. The case was initially brought to the public's attention in 2012 when Chinese company Proview Technology claimed it held the legal rights to the iPad name in China. Proview had registered the iPad trade mark in 2001 for a desktop terminal with a touch-screen display called the Internet Personal Access Device, or IPAD. The product was developed in 1998. Apple fought off the claim, stating it bought the iPad trade mark in China and nine other countries from a business owned by Proview in 2009. However, it seems that the documentation had not effectively transferred the rights to the name in China to Apple. Litigation posed a real threat to one of Apple's best-selling products.

> Proview had applied to block shipments of the tablets in and out of China which would have been disastrous given that China was, and remains, a very large market for Apple. So Apple settled the case.

The technology giant is just one of many multinational companies to have come unstuck while trying to navigate China's complex trade mark system.

Drug company Pfizer, auctioneer Sotheby's, luxury fashion house Hermes and coffee chain Starbucks are other brands that have suffered in China. While China is clearly a country which causes problems, businesses would be wise to anticipate the potential for issues surrounding rights, particularly when in the process of expanding globally.

Because many businesses fail, or never reach success, or brand owners only object to someone's use of a similar name if they are perceived to be a threat, there are fewer stories about ill-considered IP issues with SMEs than there might otherwise be. So, in many cases nobody is any the wiser.

Countless other IP problems

In this chapter I've aimed to highlight an important practical area of IP – namely the brand – because it impacts every business, and is a common issue for many.

If big household name brands with their armies of lawyers make these basic errors, it goes without saying that such errors go on all the time across the business world. The problem of lack of education in IP is the root cause of these IP errors.

The web has led to a boom in self-employment, so it is important for businesses to position themselves for success, and try to avoid problems that could derail them or cause them to waste their limited resources. That means paying attention to IP early on.

There are many other types of IP issue which a business may encounter that this chapter hasn't even touched upon. For example, you just need to consider the number of cases in the music industry where artists have tried to avoid unfavourable legal agreements, and assignments of copyright that they have agreed to, to know that ownership of copyright is another major issue for some businesses.

I met an entrepreneur who told me about a software business he had run for two years with two co-founders which folded because it emerged that the company didn't own the rights to the software. They had used a freelancer who held the rights to the software. He wanted a lot more money than they had available in order to secure an assignment of ownership to them. So the company decided to close down.

Similarly, patents and designs have given rise to numerous legal issues which any business might face. One common issue is using an ex-employee of a competitor who then creates designs for their new employer that the former employer argues infringes their IP rights. This was at the centre point of an eight-year long battle between MGA and Mattel, the owners of Barbie and Bratz.

Barbie (Mattel Inc) v Bratz dolls (MGA Entertainment)

Carter Bryant left his employment with Mattel, and was later hired by their competitor MGA, who used his work to develop Bratz dolls. A dispute arose because some of the early sketches relied on to produce Bratz were created by Bryant when he was employed by Mattel. This led to a long and heated legal battle spanning nearly a decade.

Ultimately, MGA were able to defend the lawsuit, and even won a victory of their own when they discovered that Mattel had misappropriated their trade secrets.

This is just one example of why it is vital to find out how your freelancers or consultants produced a given piece of work.

If you suspect freelancers or consultants don't have the necessary rights in their earlier work, it is safer to ask them to start over, and document everything properly. You want to own their final output. Straightforward risk management like this can reduce the risk of costly legal action further down the line. Don't underestimate the crippling effect such a dispute could have for your business, even if you are successful in litigation.

Conclusion

Any ambitious business aiming to get important things done in the world and to grow in prosperity should get early IP input, or have an IP audit, and then address its IP issues as a matter of priority.

Businesses need wide ranging IP advice which addresses not just registration of IP, but also copyright and their terms of business and other documentation too. It is never a good idea to assume that the sum total of IP involves registering your trade mark, despite the importance of names.

Visit *http://azrights.com/ip-revolution-ch9* to read reports by the UK IPO, EU IP office, and WIPO about the positive impact of IP on businesses.

Chapter 10

Limits of IP Protection

While IP is important for many of the reasons I've outlined in this book and more, it's worth noting its limitations too.

The available protections can sometimes offer very real help to a business in the bloody world of business, where competitors engage in unfair copying to pursue any new opportunities they find for making money.

Putting your legal and IP affairs in order should support your business so it can thrive and grow while avoiding pitfalls that are there for the unwary. IP also lays the foundations for scaling the business.

However, despite its many benefits, IP has limits. For example, it can't protect you against those who copy what you do – especially if they do so in another jurisdiction. Any curbs that might apply when copying another business in the same country cease to apply when the copying is by a business in another part of the globe.

Airbnb's novel business concept was quickly copied both in the USA and in other countries. Many Airbnb clones have sprung up, including Gogobot, Atraveo and SunnyRentals using similar business models to Airbnb. However, they are all operating under different names.

Distinctiveness

Having a distinctive name means that if you are one of the best at implementing a novel concept, your name will ensure the benefits of your concept and achievements are uniquely associated with your business.

Sometimes when businesses copy others they tend to adopt a similar name, logo or strapline in order to attract business towards themselves.

Asda v. Specsavers

Asda was launching its new in-store optician service. Asda's campaign included logos and colours similar to those used by Specsavers, with the logo reading 'Asda Opticians' along with tag lines like 'Be a real spec saver at Asda'. The case went all the way to the highest court in Europe, where it was held that the fact that a third party associates itself with the same colours and similar marks was enough to prove that Asda were ripping off Specsavers' distinctiveness as part of an aggressive marketing strategy. This was confirmed during the litigation proceedings where it was revealed from internal emails that Asda's marketing team had known consumers would recognise the overlapping oval logo and so Asda deliberately moved the two ovals apart to create a logo which was a 'safe distance' from Specsavers and to avoid being a 'rip off'. Unfortunately for Asda, the court did not find this sufficient to escape infringement.

To be recognisable and readily found by consumers looking for your offering provides huge protection, given the tendency in business for competitors to pile into any lucrative area of economic life. This tendency to copy is also a reason to aim to be quick to get a good idea off the ground.

It is impossible for anyone to keep a profitable niche to themselves.

Copying niches

The more lucrative an 'untouched' area of business is, the more you should expect extreme competition to quickly follow.

For example, currently Bitcoin and digital money is creating innovation and attracting investment. Businesses are vying for lucrative opportunities in the Fin Tech space. However, what is certain is that as soon as any of them hit upon a successful formula, the niche will attract competitors in droves, so that what was once a good niche, soon has an oversupply of providers. One example is Transferwise. Transferwise has enjoyed much success providing peer-to-peer money transferring services to allow people to transact globally at a fraction of the costs. They aren't the only ones, however: CurrencyFair, WeSwap, and TransferGo are arguably examples of where a market is buoyant, the competitors are quick to come. So Transferwise needs to concentrate on being better than the rest in order to stave off competition.

To prevail in whatever you do, you need to implement it well, and get a lot of other things right in the business too. A very effective protection IP can give is to stop others using similar names to divert business away from you.

As Seth Godin says of competition in *Purple Cow* (Penguin Books, 2003): 'Why do birds fly in formation? Because the birds that follow the leader have an easier flight. The leader breaks the wind resistance, and the following birds can fly far more efficiently.'

This is another way of saying that if you demonstrate a breakthrough idea, and others can see that it's a good one, they will copy it. They will benefit from the fact that you've shown them the way forward to possibly implement the idea even better than you did.

Jack Trout put it well in *Differentiate or Die* (John Wiley & Sons, 2000), when he said that being first, even if you hang around for a while, is still no guarantee of success. For example, Leica was the technology and market leader for decades in 35mm cameras until the Japanese copied German technology, improved on it, and then lowered the prices. The pioneer failed to react and ended up a bit player.

Tropicalisation

'Tropicalisation' is a term that refers to the practice of investing in start-ups which take an established business model and adapt it to an emerging market. Examples include Peixe Urbano a Brazilian clone of Groupon, which is arguably even more successful than the original; Weibo the Chinese Twitter-like microblogging platform; RenRen the Chinese version of Facebook; Baidu the Chinese take on Google; and Alibaba a Chinese copy of eBay. Alibaba is now one of the foremost online businesses.

Investors are keen on these projects as the business models are proven already and from an IP perspective there are few legal barriers to this tactic. The law does not protect bare business models, whether through patents, copyright or otherwise.

That said, cynical copying of another company's business could lead to problems if you are in the same jurisdiction, so needs care and knowhow.

Elements of a business model might be protected. For example, a patent can sometimes protect the technology which is central to a product, copyright can protect the expression of a concept, for example training and marketing materials, videos, source code and other key materials. Designs can protect the aesthetic aspects of your products, software or website, and as already discussed trade marks protect your business and product names. And securing a range of IP rights in different elements can combine to provide powerful protection.

Copyright, Patents, Designs and more

The way to have strong IP protection in your business is to secure as many IP rights as you can afford to secure because each IP right protects you in subtly different ways and situations. However, the reason why the digital world makes IP relevant to every business, is that there is a lot more to it than just IP registrations.

Often the most important IP actions will involve having the right legal agreements in place in your business. Making sure copyright issues are properly addressed, that your employment and confidentiality agreements, and terms of business are effective, plays an important part in a business' success.

Sometimes simply having secured ownership of a particular IP right through registration or contract would provide a powerful remedy enabling you to stop what copyists are doing.

Just because you have a patent over something doesn't mean you should ignore giving your business or product a distinctive name that is effective from a trade mark perspective. Securing copyright over your materials, registering the design of something like your logo, and implementing effective contracts are all important too. Each of these IP actions targets different scenarios. Until something happens in your business there is no way of knowing which of the IP rights you will need to rely on the most.

By having your IP rights adequately protected, you can rely on the most appropriate ones when the need arises. So if someone copies your logo but isn't making commercial use of it, you could use your design registration to put a stop to it. They could be using your logo in ways that can tarnish your brand – for example, featuring it on a website you do not wish to be associated with - but unless they are actually selling something using the logo you can't rely on your trade mark rights to require them to remove your logo from their site. Design registration gives you a powerful way to take action, which makes it much easier than having to rely on copyright in the logo.

There may be other undesirable practices businesses might be subjected to by competitors. For example, stealing competitive information, such as your database, or even taking your staff and using your confidential information. In all such cases you are likely to have an uphill climb during litigation unless you have taken some additional steps to protect your position. These steps may be known to IP lawyers, but may not be generally applied by their clients unless you ask your IP lawyer for help with those details. For example, a simple measure like adding a false name and address to your database could save you thousands of pounds should you ever need to prove that your database was copied by someone. However, unless you ask your lawyer for advice about how to protect your database of client information, it is unlikely you will get such nuggets of information.

Similarly, having the right contracts in place will be key to protecting your business. So although there is little you can do to prevent a competitor from creating a new business based on your concept, it would be a mistake to ignore the role of contracts in protecting your IP rights. For optimum protection you should use your IP lawyers to draft these agreements instead of assuming that contract work can be done more cheaply by a general commercial lawyer. The detail of agreements will not be the same regardless of which lawyer you use. To protect your IP position use your digital IP lawyer for all your IP needs.

Spreading ideas

In a world where the prevailing philosophy is to publish and spread your ideas to profit from them, owning copyright simply gives you a choice whether to take steps to stop copying.

Even if you are not worried enough by others copying your content to do anything about it, or do not want to get into a dispute to stop someone copying you, it still makes business sense to ensure you own the rights in products you are creating for your business, and more importantly, that you can prove your ownership.

Doing so enables you to have the choice whether to use your IP rights if someone copies you in a damaging way. It also reduces the risk of having someone else claiming ownership, and stopping your sales by claiming damages and an account of profits for infringing on their rights.

If you have a good idea, and want to ensure you implement it better than copycats who will follow, it's important to think carefully before revealing knowledge or offering up your best ideas online. Pause to consider whether your competitors might get an unfair advantage by knowing this information. Could it be that releasing your ideas too soon might give others the opportunity to beat you to the punch?

It really does depend on the idea as to how important it is to keep it confidential. For example, if you intend to set up a website to make it easier for businesses to offer a monthly payment subscription facility (for example, the Go Cardless business model), it is highly unlikely that giving this top level information would expose you to the risk of someone else beating you to the punch. That's because there is so much else involved to get this concept off the ground. The barriers to entry seem high too in that you need a certain level of knowledge to be able to make use of the idea. So, it may not be necessary to guard the mere idea and keep it a secret. On the other hand, if your idea is something which anyone could implement without industry and specialist knowledge, then you might need to be more protective of it.

Being smart about how and when and whether to release know-how and ideas is an important aspect of under-standing IP and its limitations. You want to get exposure without seriously disadvantaging yourself.

Generally, this means allowing sufficient lead time to bring your ideas to fruition before revealing them.

Early promotion may be useful to drum up interest, but if you misjudge the timing you could simply give com-petitors your good ideas and miss an opportunity to lead the market if they were to run with your idea before you had a chance to implement and develop it. On the other hand, it's important to be realistic about what competi-tors could or might do, and in what timescales. Only you can be the judge of what to publish and when, but you need to temper your fears with a large dose of realism.

Why owning IP rights is similar to buying property

SMEs should adopt the same matter-of-fact approach to owning IP rights and avoiding IP infringement as they would when buying physical property. You don't go through the legal steps involved just so you can sue someone should they trespass on your land.

Your motivation is more to own the property so you can enjoy it peacefully, sell it in future, maybe at an increased value. Similarly, you don't want someone else to turn up along the line claiming that you're squatting on their property. It's exactly the same with IP rights. In this digital world when the principal assets of a business are its intangibles, taking the right actions to secure rights to your intangible property is the smart thing to do.

Use of NDAs

While non-disclosure agreements (NDAs) protect you, don't take too much comfort from the mere signing of a confidentiality agreement. Not all situations merit the same type of NDA. Many projects involve other contractual provisions, and these would entail appropriate restrictions too, not just a requirement to maintain confidentiality. For example, you may want to restrict your web designer from outsourcing the major part of the work on Elance or other platforms.

It's unlikely that potential investors would be willing to sign NDAs. It's more to your advantage that they hear what you have to say than it is to theirs. That's because, statistically, there are a lot more people looking for investment than there are investors. However, if you have an idea which the relevant person could implement better than you, then don't talk to them for investment.

If you have written a document containing sensitive price information and market insights, disclosing the document to a third party under an obligation of confidentiality increases your protection. That is because you can rely both on copyright infringement and breach of confidence, depending on what happens in the future, to stop undesirable use of your information.

An example is the Winklevoss twins' legal battle with Mark Zuckerburg over the concept of Facebook.

The Winklevoss twins claimed that they had created the concept for Facebook. They had to argue their case in court against Mark Zuckerburg who allegedly created the now 1.44-billion-user network after discussing the idea with the Winklevoss twins under an obligation of confidentiality. Although the Winklevosses were able to reach a settlement for $65 million, it bears no comparison with the net worth of the company which is closer to $50 billion.

If you have a potentially lucrative idea, the best thing is probably not to tell anyone. However, if you need to communicate the information to a third party in order to progress it, make sure you use a confidentiality agreement, defining what information is commercially sensitive and/ or confidential. This is crucial to any information, the dissemination of which you want to be able to control.

If the other party took so much detail from your document that it could be argued they had copied a substantial part of it, you may be able to argue that they infringed your copyright by copying it.

Conclusion

In conclusion there are limits to what IP can protect, but the law is there to protect a business in certain situations that might arise.

If you secure IP rights, you may never need to use them in litigation because many savvy businesses will take note of your rights, and not infringe them. So, it is misguided to think of IP rights as only worth having if you can afford to go to court to defend them. And the fact that IP rights have limits and can't protect you in some of the ways outlined in this chapter, should not be used as a reason for not securing any IP protection at all.

Visit *http://azrights.com/ip-revolution-ch10* to download a sample Non-disclosure Agreement.

Part Four

Global Nature of IP

Chapter 11

International IP System and Domains

IP laws are territorial; the web is borderless.

What this means is that your IP rights are limited to the country or countries in which you register or use them. On the other hand, your business will be accessible internationally so it's necessary to think globally about domain and IP registrations.

If you sell online, even though you may just operate out of a bedroom in your home, you are doing business worldwide. So the need to take account of the international dimension arises immediately.

The law has always been slow to catch up with new technology and developments, and nowhere is this more evident than on the web. The territorial nature of IP rights sits poorly with the global nature of ecommerce business.

Unlike many other areas of law, IP laws have to work on an international level so as to afford adequate protection. Therefore, there are a number of agreements in place between states on the subject of IP to achieve this objective.

History

As countries gradually realised that their IP laws were unable to protect their citizens against freeloading competitors based abroad, they began to cooperate by making international agreements. Initially, this started as two countries combining forces to address problems that their citizens were experiencing.

For example, in the eighteenth century, the UK discovered that many of its authors' works were being reproduced abroad without permission and that they were not receiving any royalties on them. Much of the 'piracy' was taking place in the United States, where authors like Dickens were very popular with the public and therefore with US publishers.

The British response was to pass legislation in the mid-19th century protecting works first published outside the UK provided the relevant state in which the author of the work was resident reciprocated by protecting UK works. This resulted in a considerable number of bilateral agreements between the UK and other states.

However, this bilateral approach did not give satisfactory protection to authors and eventually led to two multilateral approaches: the Paris and Berne Conventions (1883 and 1886 respectively). The Paris Convention was aimed at 'industrial property' (what we now call intellectual property) while the Berne Convention was predominantly focused on the protection of literary and artistic works (copyright).

These agreements were open for signature and ratification by the world at large. By signing up to them, a country agreed to the principle of 'national treatment', and recognition of a set of minimum rights for foreign works.

National treatment is a principle in international law which means treating foreigners and locals equally. Under its terms, if a signatory to one of these Conventions grants a particular right, benefit or privilege to its own citizens, it must also grant those advantages to the citizens of other states while they are in that country. This is why if you come from a country such as the UK (which does not have a registration system for copyright works), your work can benefit from copyright protection in a country that does have a requirement for copyright registration.

These international initiatives eventually gave rise to the creation of what is now the international organization known as the World Intellectual Property Organization (WIPO). States signing up to WIPO were not agreeing to harmonize their technical rules so much as to give national treatment.

In other words, states retain enormous discretion over the IP standards that they set internally. Until recently, the United States for example, continued with its 'first to invent' patent system, while other countries operate under a 'first to file' patent system.

Civil code countries (many European countries are based on such codes) continue to adopt the doctrine of moral rights for authors, while common law countries (such as the UK and former Commonwealth countries) place more emphasis on the exclusive right to exploit a work, which copyright gives an author.

Countries have also joined forces and signed up to treaties and conventions, such as the World Trade Organization (WTO)) and the Agreement on Trade-Related Aspects of Intellectual Property Rights (TRIPS) which goes a long way towards harmonising laws.

Although states are not required to have the same laws on IP, the way the TRIPS system works is that participating countries are required to have a set of mandatory minimum standards. These standards may be implemented in different ways by each country's national laws because many aspects and details are left to their discretion.

So, TRIPS sets up a mechanism which monitors members' compliance with their obligations under the Agreement, and checks whether their IP laws comply.

In the next chapter I will look at how these work in practice, while here it would be useful to look at domain names which are intrinsically international given that they are designed for the internet.

Domain names provide a good example of why you need to be strategic and consider your approach to registration in other countries early on.

So, what is involved in internationalising your domains?

Domains

A consideration that is related to the name you use is what domains to register and when to buy further domains.

For example, a UK ecommerce business might typically start by registering a co.uk, .com, and .net domain. These will be relatively inexpensive, but should you also register other Country Code Top Level Domains (CCTLDs)? If, say, France is a market to which you will sell, should you also register a '.fr' name, and if China is important to you should you buy a '.cn' name, too?

As your business grows and you get customers in other countries you will need to consider whether to buy your domain name in other country codes.

There are more than 250 country code domain names. It would be too expensive to buy your name in all of them. The strategic considerations will differ for every business. Typically, many wait until their business starts to take off before looking at more extensive domain registrations.

The key is always to look at where you are doing business or might be doing business soon. The priority is to register in those markets in which you have customers or in which you think you will be selling in the near future.

Unlike the GTLDs — generic top-level domain names, - .com, .net, .org - where there's a lot of uniformity, the rules for country codes are different in every country, as are the prices. Sometimes you need a trade mark to get a registration. Other times you need a local business registration. And in some cases you may need a local presence or a local address. So, the CCTLDs usually cost more.

Cybersquatting

One aspect of domain name considerations is what happens if someone in another country steals your name and registers your domain with the local CCTLD? This is called cybersquatting. What can you do about it?

The strategy for registering domains needs to bear in mind that it may be difficult to block another person from using your name in another country. Therefore, your strategy needs to be combined with your trade mark registration strategy.

Your remedies for the individual CCTLDs sometimes depend on whether or not the name you are using is trade marked. It will also depend on the country's dispute resolution policies. Each country has different dispute policies, and different procedures for granting relief.

For example, in the UK the dispute resolution body that deals with .co.uk issues is Nominet. This organisation will typically consider whether you have trade mark rights (which does not necessarily entail having a registered trade mark, although it is a lot simpler if you do have a registration), and whether the registration or the use of the domain name is in 'bad faith'. That is, whether the person who registered it likely did so in order to resell it to the person who has the name or in order to divert revenue to themselves for economic gain.

The first step in these administrative style dispute procedures is to file a complaint. There is no court involved as it's an arbitration. Once you've complained, the other party must answer the complaint and the arbiter then decides whether or not the person against whom you have complained should be able to keep the domain name or should release the name into your ownership. The decision is purely based on the pleadings. You don't have a day in court.

For other domains, such as .com the registry designate groups such as the World Intellectual Property Organization (WIPO) or the National Arbitration Forum or other groups to decide the dispute.

These arbitration groups have a lot of experience and history in handling domain disputes.

So access to good specialist advice is key as is being strategic about where you register domains. This will partly be dependent on the rules of the different countries. For example, if a local business registration is needed in order to register a domain, you might decide the risk of cybersquatting is low, and perhaps just register a trade mark.

Once you've taken all the issues into consideration, you should end up with a priority list based on the intrinsic risks.

Difficulty obtaining information in order to register IP in other markets

Given the impact the web has on businesses in terms of the global nature of the IP issues they need to address I think it might be useful to consider how a business might go about internationalising its IP.

The majority of established businesses, particularly those that don't have a large portfolio of brands and other IP, will turn to their IP advisers for international protection. Often domains will not be included in the brief as the founders address these themselves or delegate to their web designers. As there is a lot to know about domains, and they are closely related to your trade mark rights, I would recommend including domains in the brief to IP lawyers, and not entrusting them to web designers. Like that, your IP lawyers can more readily take in the complete picture.

Some businesses prefer to engage IP lawyers in other countries directly rather than instructing them through a single IP lawyer in overall charge of their brand issues. It may seem more cost effective to pursue this option, although I would not recommend it. You need a specialist to manage lawyers in other countries for you, to ensure you are using lawyers with the right skills, and most importantly that you achieve consistency in your IP protection.

Some early stage businesses may be on such a tight budget that they will try to do their own legal work.

Whether you are an in-house legal department of a business looking to engage IP professionals in other countries, or a company doing its own sourcing of IP professionals in other countries, it's important to be aware of the issues involved in finding reliable and trustworthy service providers who will do a good job cost effectively.

This is especially the case given that it can sometimes take several years to secure registration in some countries. I often meet other lawyers at international conferences; chatting to one of them, I learned that when using a lawyer in another country, a lawyer was given many excuses as to why there had been no news on an application the local agent was progressing. In the end the lawyer made enquiries and discovered that the local agent was not regulated by any professional body and had missed a deadline. The client's registration had not been processed. Worse still, the lawyer had simply asked around when looking for an IP firm in that country, and had not done any due diligence checks on the company simply because another IP professional had suggested them. He wasappalled to discover that the agent running the business was not regulated so there was very little comeback.

This brought home the importance of picking service providers that are properly qualified, and reliable, and who are regulated, so that there is some recourse if you're unlucky enough to use an unreliable service provider.

In many countries, including the UK, there are no laws stopping anyone from offering their services as an IP registration company. For example, in the UK apart from IP solicitors, trade mark and patent attorney firms, you will find a range of others offering IP registration services. They might be former clerks who have had little experience of the law, and have set up in business after leaving a law firm where they might have learned a little bit about trade mark registration. These organisations are often quick to find as they use Google Ads and other methods of advertising to get clients. They often have good sales skills, and may charge low rates. Some people therefore use them.

It can be a big risk to do business with entities that are not under the overall control of a regulatory body, so I would advise only using providers who are regulated. I always look for generally qualified lawyers – the equivalent of IP solicitors in this country. That is people who have formal qualifications, and are subject to regulation by an official body. I will then check out the company to ensure it is registered with the body in question.

There are many scams in the IP world too, whereby companies write to people whose names are on the official IP registers, sending them official looking invoices in relation to a recent filing their company made. Many such entities are located in far flung places or are EU-based companies. Some even justify their business model as legitimate by arguing that they are offering a genuine service, despite a ruling by the Advertising Standards Board that their sending out what looked like an invoice from the official registration body was misleading. However, it does not stop these fly-by-night companies from continuing to operate. They are such a problem that the UK IPO and OHIM regularly send out warning notices about them.

In this climate you can't be too careful who you entrust with your registration work, whether in this country or abroad.

Checking that a registration has in fact been undertaken

I've even come across someone who believed his company had a registered trade mark because he had paid a third party to secure registration. He had received a certificate and assumed his mark was registered. He only became aware that he had been conned and did not have a registration when I queried his use of the ® symbol as his company was not on the trade mark register. Needless to say, the entity he had used to secure 'registration' was nowhere to be found.

In conclusion, the search for service providers directly in other countries can be a minefield to navigate. The first issue is ensuring the service provider is regulated, and genuine. Then it is often necessary to find two or three such providers in order to get a few quotes given the wide variation in prices. Legal fees vary enormously between different firms. Price is just one consideration when getting quotes though. Often you are also looking at the totality of your interactions with the firm to assess whether they are suitable agents to work with. For example, we look to work with agents who do not charge hourly rate fees, and who will first forewarn us before charging us further fees. This is so we can avoid surprising our clients with invoices they were not expecting.

There is the added difficulty of getting to grips with the rules in a given country. For example, in some countries there is a need for legalisation and notarisation of documents which can considerably add to the costs.

On top of this, some legal systems are founded on a different basis, such as a single class application system in Canada. Others, such as China, may involve the need to file separate applications for each class, and to consider whether to file a local language version of the mark too.

So, it can be a time consuming and complex exercise just to get a quote for a single country. And the quote will only cover the application. Understanding whether or not there are further charges down the line can be equally complex as it depends on the law firm's working practices, and the local custom of the IP trade mark registry in a given country. It's very possible that what looks like a cheaper quote from one provider might in fact be a much higher one when you bear in mind the further charges which one of them will impose down the line.

Conclusion

On the one hand, it is important to think globally, and register rights in other markets too. And on the other hand, it can be difficult for companies to compare like with like when getting quotes so as to be able to use their resources effectively.

Yet it is necessary to avoid infringing on the rights of others and to secure important rights in other markets so that your IP rights are protected in key markets abroad. There will be different considerations as to the registrations that a pharmaceutical or food company may need to secure compared to an online ecommerce store. What is for sure, is that the issue should be addressed and planned for, otherwise it has the potential to result in costly, and time consuming mistakes.

Visit *http://azrights.com/ip-revolution-ch11/* to find out more about the international agreements in place to facilitate your wider IP protection globally.

Chapter 12

Internationalising IP

In view of the global nature of the web, it's necessary to adopt an international perspective when considering intellectual property laws. This is because if you have customers in different countries, you are using your trade mark in those territories. So questions about whether you might be infringing on somebody else's trade mark rights within a particular territory, and whether to register your mark in other markets, arise early on.

The current international trade mark system was designed for a very different business environment, one that's more suited to the pocket of well-resourced, well-funded multinationals that gradually move into new markets internationally.

A small business may struggle to find the financial resources to internationalise its IP registrations everywhere from the outset. Yet it is important to be strategic about it, so as to not neglect to register in other countries when the implications could be disastrous, as this next case illustrates.

Plenty of Fish v. Plenty More Fish

Plentyoffish.com was a well-established online dating site for many years when PlentyMoreFish.com set up a competing online business based in the UK, and applied to register a trade mark in the UK.

Plenty of Fish wanted to stop Plenty More Fish from creating customer confusion and benefiting from the reputation it had built up online. It decided to oppose Plenty More Fish's UK trade mark application.

The only reason Plenty More Fish was able to set up a competing service using a similar name was that it based its business in the UK and applied to register a trade mark in the UK. The global village environment of the web, and its lack of territorial boundaries, was to its advantage because it could divert some of Plenty of Fish's business to itself (simply due to the confusion between the two similar names).

Had both businesses been based within the same territorial borders, it would have amounted to passing off and trade mark infringement to set up a competing business to that of an established player by using a similar name. However, as Plenty of Fish was a web business, the question of whether Plenty of Fish had rights in the UK to prevent Plenty More Fish from registering a trade mark turned on whether it had customers in the UK. If it did have customers there, it would have had 'earlier rights' in the UK and may have been successful in opposing Plenty More Fish's trade mark application and prevent its use of a similar name.

As the company did not have any subscribers in the UK, it was unable to prevent Plenty More Fish from using a similar name online and registering a UK trade mark.

The international application of IP laws is relevant to online businesses at a much earlier stage than before, and founders and company executives need access to advice about the way the IP system works internationally.

It's essential to discover not only whether an IP right, such as a name, is available to use in all your intended markets, but also to establish whether it is legally effective (that is, whether it can function as a trade mark). What you don't want is to have a local business use your brand to block you from selling to their local market by using their trade mark rights against you.

International schemes

As countries have joined forces and signed up to treaties and conventions, a number of international procedures are available to help companies to secure protection of their IP in certain other countries using a single application.

The most well-known example of this is the Patent Co-operation Treaty (PCT) whereby it is possible to extend the life of a patent application. The initial patent filing gives you protection for twelve months worldwide. By filing a PCT application before the twelve months are up, you can extend the international protection for a further eighteen months in those countries that are party to the PCT, which for most practical purposes, means globally.

Once you have extended the application and paid the official fees, this gives you a further eighteen months, within which to decide on the countries to designate for patent protection. The fees tend to get higher once you designate countries, and you have to start paying translation fees too, so the international single application procedure is useful to extend the life of your application while you are still assessing the commercial potential of your patent.

A similar option exists under the Madrid system for trade marks which is discussed at length below, and there is also a single application procedure for designs under the Hague Convention.

As trade marks are the most universally applicable form of IP, I will now consider them in more detail.

Madrid System

Trade marks share some similarities worldwide even though each country's laws differ as they originate from different philosophical and legal traditions. While the details of the law vary from country to country, it is possible to secure trade mark protection in several countries using a single application. The Madrid system provides a simple way to achieve this for those countries that are party to the system.

There are many advantages in registering through the Madrid system in terms of ease of administration, cost savings and flexibility.

The trade mark registries of the countries specified in your application have eighteen months in which to raise any objections to your application. If none are raised, your application is deemed accepted.

Once you apply under the Madrid system, if objections are raised in any given country, your mark will not be accepted there unless you are able to overcome the objections. Overcoming the objections would involve engaging the services of a local lawyer in that country who would have the necessary 'rights of audience' to correspond with the foreign registry. So, although there isn't the administrative burden involved when you use the Madrid system, which I discussed in the previous chapter, of finding service providers in each country, it is necessary to find providers if objections are raised to your application.

If your application fails in any of your desired countries, it will still be acceptable in other countries unless there are valid objections raised against it in any of those countries too.

The way the Madrid system works is that you first apply to register a UK or EU trade mark, assuming those are the areas in which you do business. You then have a priority right for up to six months to extend your trade mark protection to many other countries worldwide covering the same mark. In this way it is possible to secure your rights in jurisdictions with very different legal systems, and to do so by filing an application from your home country. The desired country just needs to be party to the Madrid Protocol.

Searching internationally

If someone in another country is using the same (or a similar) name for a similar line of business, then you would not be within your rights to use your brand in their country. Due to the international scope of the web, any business selling to an online audience should therefore check that their chosen name may be used internationally.

If you intend to use the same name worldwide, then you must check that it's available internationally before committing to that name. Then you should have a strategy for determining when to register a trade mark in other countries, focusing on your most important markets first.

So once you've applied for a UK or EU trade mark, provided you go on to file for trade mark protection in your desired territories within six months, you may claim priority over third parties who may apply to register a similar name in those countries in the meantime.

This is a time-limited right that is triggered by the first filing of an application, and is granted by virtue of international treaties between countries discussed earlier.

However, it is not completely fool proof, as we'll see below, but is a good enough basis for protecting a trade mark in jurisdictions that matter to you without having to incur the costs of international applications as soon as you start up with a new name.

'First to file' or 'first to use'?

Many countries determine priority of trade mark rights on a 'first-to-file' for registration basis rather than on a 'first-to-adopt-and-use' basis.

Some first-to-file trade mark systems include China, France, Germany, Japan, and Spain. The United States is a first-to-adopt-and-use country.

In first-to-file countries, prior use is not a prerequisite to registering a trade mark. Also, in first-to-file countries, use of the mark (without a registration) will not provide priority trade mark rights.

So there is literally a race to the trade mark offices in those countries with a first-to-file registration system, and prompt applications for registration are critical for protection of trade marks in those countries.

Bear this in mind when relying on the six-month priority right for international registration. Consider whether you want to reduce the risks by filing for protection immediately in any first-to-file country that represents a significant market for your brand.

Why registering in other territories is important

A case which illustrates the importance of filing trade mark applications in other countries as your business begins to expand is Lexia (a fictitious name to protect the identity of the parties).

Lexia

This UK-based ecommerce site had been selling its products in the United States for more than eight years without having registered a trade mark there. A competitor then set up a bricks and mortar shop in the United States selling similar products and also called itself Lexia. The original Lexia company was alerted to this when publicity surrounding the new shop was spotted by one of its existing customers who emailed to congratulate it on its new venture in California.

Lexia had to engage lawyers to file a trade mark application in the United States. After hefty costs and legal correspondence, the US attorneys successfully secured a US registration for Lexia. This was achieved because of the numerous customers that the company had in the United States and in California. US trade mark rules gave the original Lexia prior rights in the name.

The company could have avoided the hefty legal fees if it had registered its mark in the United States as soon as it began selling its products there.

Registering rights in other countries

As official fees can be very high, some businesses are tempted to dispense with expert help, to do their own IP registrations. This is particularly likely if the company has its own in-house lawyers who could do the work.

A word of warning here is that the first application you file is extremely important. If it is not well drafted and properly scoped, all your subsequent international applications will suffer from the same defect. That's because they are likely to be based on this initial application. The Madrid system certainly uses your initial base UK or EU application and extends it to other countries. The same applies to patents.

If you're intending to do your own international application, it is worth getting the base application professionally produced, and paying for advice so you can develop your individual strategy to registering rights in other markets internationally. Thereafter, it is possible to secure protection elsewhere more cost effectively by doing the work yourself as it is largely an administrative exercise.

Conclusion

The difficulty of finding well qualified, expert lawyers in other countries is overcome when the countries in which you wish to extend your protection are party to a single application process like the Madrid Protocol, the Hague

Convention, and the Patent Co-Operation Treaty. That's as far as making the application goes. If once you've applied a registry raises objections, then you would need local lawyers in that country to help you deal with the matter.

There are still many countries that are not party to these agreements, so it will be necessary to find service providers in these other jurisdictions to make the initial applications. Additionally, even despite the existence of these treaties, it may be cheaper to file directly in a country.

These are just some of the challenges of registering IP rights globally.

Visit *http://azrights.com/ip-revolution-ch12* to use our Madrid Protocol Fee Calculator to find out the cost of the official fees to register in countries of your choice.

Conclusion

Digital IP Market and Legal Services

My aim in writing this book is to highlight how the web has revolutionised the subject of intellectual property, so it is of central relevance to every business, whether pre start-up or mature.

Given that digital business is intangible it is not surprising that the law which deals with intangibles, namely IP law, is now so key. What is surprising is that this has yet to be recognised in society generally.

The IP industry is increasingly fragmented. There is a bewildering choice of practitioners who are apparently the natural choice for IP matters–patent attorneys, trade mark attorneys, IP, corporate and commercial solicitors and barristers, as well as non-lawyers providing IP-related services. As a result, IP help has never been so inaccessible at a time when it is needed the most.

SMEs' needs for wider digital IP services is largely unaddressed. Every ambitious business must identify its IP issues early on and consider how best to manage and protect that IP. That is the way to build a valuable business, should it succeed.

While businesses with an internet presence will all have a name or a logo by way of traditional registrable headline IP, most of them will have a multitude of other IP issues to also consider. This might involve properly protecting know how and trade secrets, or commissioning websites, or using appropriate terms of business, privacy policies, employment agreements, and more. These are all critical to the IP protection and management needed to build value. So, why are the authorities routinely directing SMEs to patent and trade mark attorney firms, many of whom are not equipped to address these wider IP needs?

The needs of SMEs

Due to the current confused IP landscape, legal issues can and do fall between the cracks. Under the present system you are expected to visit several different firms for IP help, which in practice many SMEs simply don't do.

The Clementi report highlighted the lack of adequate, affordable access to copyright advice. Consequently, civil servants in the IPO are being trained to plug the gap, but this is unlikely to adequately deal with the wide-ranging legal issues raised in this book.

Either SMEs still don't know how important it is to cover IP properly, or they do not know to whom to turn for effective, affordable help. Currently, what often falls by the wayside is digital IP issues, such as website development, privacy policies and other commercial considerations relevant to websites, as well as copyright and internet law matters.

More seriously, there is little advice available to enable SMEs to think strategically about their name choice, and marry it with appropriate guidance on domain names and search engine optimisation. Instead they are led to mistakenly believe that any name they use in their business is good enough provided they register it as a trade mark. Worse still, they are encouraged to file their own trade marks. This means nobody is alerting them to the fact that the very choice of name is an issue on which it is vital to take advice.

So, it's important for SMEs to know that the way the law protects a company's competitive advantage is through its name.

The role of names in protecting your competitive position

If a company has innovated in its field by developing a product or service which becomes well known in the market, the name by which that product is recognised is how the product attracts enquiries and sales.

Assuming the underlying concept is freely copyable, and is not protected with a patent, it will inevitably attract copycat 'me too' offerings from competitors. That is the reality in business when a product is a good idea, meets a market need, and has low barriers to entry.

The product's name can create a strong barrier to entry against copycat offerings if it is well chosen. That is the one thing competitors can't take away, if it is distinctive and uniquely owned by the business.

Where a company with a highly successful product has given that product a name that purely describes the service, it will enjoy little distinctiveness in the market, and will be vulnerable to copycats offering similar products using similar names. Many businesses in that unfortunate position are surprised to learn how limited their protection is against unscrupulous competitors.

Sometimes SMEs in such a position point to their trade mark registration and wonder why competitors are able to use the same name as them. They assume that the purely descriptive name included in their combined name and logo trade mark belongs to them, and that they should be able to stop competitors using the same name.

However, in fact, where the name is purely descriptive and is registered as a combined logo mark, what is protected is the logo not the name. The registration gave them a false sense of security and this happens because society is sending out the message that you need to register a trade mark. Instead the message should be that you need to get advice on your choice of name because it has significant ramifications for your business and the value it will attract if the business succeeds.

The company using a purely descriptive name does not have an IP asset that is capable of protecting its competitive position. Competitors will be able to start delivering a similar service using similar names with the result that the company's name recognition will be inadequate to protect its asset (the successful product), and therefore it will make fewer sales once competitors enter the market. This inevitably means its value will be diminished.

When you realise what makes a name legally effective, and how the legal system approaches the protection of names, you will better appreciate which names might potentially protect a company's IP assets.

Names are only perfect if they are both legally available and legally effective. Then it is possible to prevent copyists using similar names to describe their competing offerings and divert business to themselves.

How distinctive names protect your offering

The company that first introduced a successful product will enjoy more enquiries due to having a distinctive name, and as a result will have a higher value. Competitors are not free to enter the market with a competing product and advertise it as being similar to the market leader's product. Doing so risks infringing the market leader's trade mark. So they inevitably take longer to establish themselves as a recognised alternative.

In an increasingly global market it is not enough to simply register a UK or EU trade mark. It's important to secure registrations in all markets where the business has customers because the name protects its competitive position.

Before leaving this topic I should stress that names are not the only form of IP that protect a company's competitive position. Sometimes it might be a patent, other times it might be a trade secret, or a database that is the key asset of a business. There is no one size fits all. Some people assume that trade mark registration is all there is to IP. Others believe that the choice of name doesn't matter as long as it can be registered as a trade mark, somehow. As mentioned, in the above example not all registrations are equal. A combined mark might be worthless as a way to protect a business' unique offering, if it effectively protects just the logo.

Another trap for the unwary with names is that registrations are capable of being challenged. People often register trade marks without doing adequate due diligence checks, unaware that trade mark owners do not lose their right to object to the registration just because they let the registration proceed to registration. Trade marks can be made the subject of cancellation proceedings down the line. So, an important aspect of addressing the IP of a business is to have searches carried out to assess whether someone else has a better right to the name or other IP that the business has registered or is using.

Although, in theory, it is possible to do due diligence without turning to a professional, it's important to appreciate the added value that a professional offers. Being able to rely on the results of the due diligence is fundamental. That is how you can make any changes or adjustments to ensure you build more value in your business.

Foundations of sand

For these and similar reasons, it is possible that some businesses that appear very successful are built on a house of cards. There may be a façade of perfection, but when you get beneath the surface you may find it doesn't match up to the reality.

Building a business without a solid legal foundation in place inevitably involves being in a near constant state of fear, and potentially having to deal with all sorts of impossible challenges and conflicts.

But it's not just about the risk of unwittingly stepping on others' toes that is the concern. There is the very real point to bear in mind that IP assets underpin a business' future revenue streams, as indicated in the chapter on licensing and franchising.

Identifying and Protecting IP Assets

A commitment to addressing the issues a business may be neglecting, and dealing with them is key to building a valuable business. One way to begin to tackle any gaps is to have a comprehensive IP audit.

However, not all IP audits are the same. Many of them tend to focus the main attention on traditional forms of IP like patents, trade marks and designs which are capable of being registered. Many ignore digital issues because the type of firms offering IP audits are not well versed in internet law.

Informal IP is incapable of registration so tends not to get much attention in IP audits. Yet it is equally important in maintaining or driving a company's competitive advantage. It still can and should be protected. Trade secrets, one of the informal IP rights, is a viable alternative to patent applications, as mentioned earlier in the book. It merits a robust trade secrets policy in order to prevent trade secret leakage. Coca Cola's secret recipe is one of the most famous examples of a trade secret that is well protected against discovery by a competitor. Other informal rights, such as critical customer, supplier and partner relationships, can enhance the value in a company's brand and reputation, whereas organisational knowledge and business processes can make a company more valuable in the eyes of prospective investors and buyers. They can therefore help your business realise a greater valuation on exit.

Getting good quality advice so as to take stock of your IP is essential if you have ambitions for your business.

One benefit in doing so is that you are better able to capture value and build wealth if your business is successful. Another advantage is that you avoid disaster such as can happen when a business has not taken stock of its IP and structured it correctly.

In one case a company unwittingly sold off critically important IP, a piece of software held in a group company, when it sold one of its subsidiaries. In another case, a company didn't realise that one of its important brand names was registered by the subsidiary it sold off, causing many undesirable and costly repercussions for the business.

As well as wanting to ensure your IP is held in the right way so as to ward off such risks, you should find out how to appropriately manage and protect your key IP assets.

It never makes sense to gamble with your future. Get proper advice to identify and manage your IP assets so you can build your business on strong foundations and guard against the risk of unwittingly infringing on the rights of others.

What every business wants to avoid is the risk of being hit by a sudden, expensive claim which could cause the business to fail.

IP should push you forwards not hold you back

IP presents risks and opportunities. Taking IP risks that are readily manageable with a proper IP strategy in place could have severe downsides.

Growth and success depend on the IP embodied in the products and services you sell, and in the IP that protects your competitive advantage. Learn how to commercialise your assets, and make sure you truly own the IP your business relies on.

Final words

As more and more businesses nowadays are knowledge-based entities providing services, an important aspect of exploiting their knowledge and turning it into IP assets, is to create product-style service offerings.

We have done this at Azrights. For example, we have developed offerings to review your IP and obtain essential protection for a fixed price. The deliverables are indicated in advance. They might comprise a meeting, letter of advice, trade mark or other registration, contractual documentation. The outcome is that your IP is identified and key steps taken to protect it by securing initial registrations and implementing legal documentation. There is complete price certainty, and you know in advance what extra charges there may be. For example, the price might include trade mark registration in three classes and if you need more than this then you know how much you would need to pay to get more classes.

This is very different to the way the legal industry charges for services. It may superficially look as though everyone offers a fixed price because all law firms will quote a price. However, most law firms are just giving you an estimated price based on their hourly rates and the number of hours they believe the job will take them. Then you get charged more (or less) than this depending on how long the work actually takes the firm to do.

At Azrights we are different. We have turned our business around so as to offer many services at a set price. The client buys the value and benefits to be delivered, regardless of how long the work takes us to do. We are able to give price certainty by saying in advance what is or isn't included. Clients know what they're buying, and can decide whether to buy additional services as and when the need arises.

This is the approach I would recommend other law firms and knowledge businesses adopt if they want to build assets in their business. If you embed the knowledge into an IT system you can build a really valuable asset of the business which will deliver revenues with fewer people needing to be involved in the delivery. So, the business is able to make more money from its knowledge, and do it more cost effectively than through the traditional one-to-one consultancy services that is typical in law firms.

By avoiding offering your knowledge in return for the time it takes you, you can build more wealth. It will also increase the value of your business.

So, any service based business should consider how it can turn its services into a product-style offering that delivers known benefits at a known price. The price certainty for clients is much more attractive.

This is one of the ways we are able to help our clients–we go far beyond just considering traditional forms of IP.

I wrote this book to highlight why IP is relevant to every size of business in the digital world. If your plans involve the internet or technology, then I hope you will now be aware of the importance of getting very early IP input, and having a digital IP lawyer on your team.

IP has a potentially transformative effect on a business. It is the heart of your business, and can make a great difference to the value you build if your business is a success. I hope this book has given a sense of its relevance, and importance.

Appendix

The Impact of the Digital Revolution on the Legal Industry

The emergence of the web and the technologies which facilitated user generated content and social media have impacted every industry. Whether you are an online or offline business, the discussions taking place online impact your business. People are making recommendations, adding reviews about businesses and freely airing their views online.

According to many writers on the subject, we have yet to experience the exponential development of technologies that are on the horizon.

In the meantime, the web is revolutionising society and the business models of every industry, including the law. Before looking at the legal industry it is useful to consider how the print industry is experiencing these changes.

Print media industry

The plethora of free news source has changed our habits forever. For example, who buys newspapers nowadays? Consequently, the print media industry is grappling with the implications of a decline in newspaper sales.

The industry has yet to find a business model to make up for this lost income.

While the price of newspapers alone never underpinned a profitable publication, the ad revenue which impacted profitability has also been affected by our changing habits.

Nowadays few of us consult the *Yellow Pages* when we look for products and services. The first port of call for many of us is Google or another search engine.

This phenomenon means businesses have new ways to reach consumers. Blogging and social media are proving to be prime ways to communicate with consumers and to better understand customer needs.

Blogs, online news sources, social media, and other forms of web content give buyers information at the time when they want it. They no longer tolerate being interrupted with promotional messages while they are doing something else (like watching a TV program). This is why people are charged a higher price on platforms like Spotify if they don't want advertisements to interrupt their listening.

This has had a deep impact on the advertising business model. The challenge for marketing and advertising is to find new ways to convey a message to consumers, now that we tend to filter out advertising messages.

Nowadays promotional content might be placed on social media, on dedicated sites, or with bloggers who have a large readership. So, there is less reliance on traditional print media outlets for advertising. This further impacts the revenues of the print media industry.

The Times newspapers has approached the drop in circulation revenue by setting up pay walls. This inevitably has its downsides in reducing the paper's exposure. Others, such as the *Guardian* who have chosen to make their news freely available, have benefited by getting more than 84 million unique monthly visitors.

Nevertheless, the *Guardian* is still looking for alternative income streams. It has yet to succeed in offsetting the lost offline newspaper sales. Those free views are seriously cutting into the magazine's profits, and despite positioning the paper as one of the most popular publications online, advertising revenues have not made up for those lost sales.

According to the paper's CEO, Andrew Miller, it is unlikely that the paper can continue to sustain the level of losses it is experiencing and may have to cease its current operations in the United Kingdom.

So, the print media industry is still challenged to make the web work to its advantage. How is the legal industry faring in this changed climate?

The web shakes up the legal field

The legal sector is under pressure due to shifting customer behaviours and habits.

Technology is democratising access to knowledge and information, of which lawyers used to be the guardians. This means people are not paying for legal advice so much nowadays. When you want to know the answer to a legal query, you look for it online first. If Google delivers a good enough answer, depending on what you wanted to know, you might decide not to consult a lawyer.

Back in the 90s when I wanted to do a trade mark search, it was necessary to visit the Patent Office off Chancery Lane in person. Contrast that with the situation now where access to the Intellectual Property Offices of the UK and many other countries is available at your fingertips.

Client expectations

The fact that there is a wealth of information on the web, in turn impacts client expectations.

One business owner I spoke to told me he had decided to move away from his firm of patent and trade mark attorneys because they were charging him a sum of money just to renew his European design registration that he perceived to be too high. He had worked out how to do it for himself, and was appalled that the firm was charging him several hundred pounds for something which he was able to achieve himself in a few minutes.

These forces influence prices and costs.

Given that information is freely available, Azrights tends to give information away freely in books, articles, and blogs. However, if a new enquirer wants one-to-one time either because it will be quicker than sifting through the information in our blogs and books, or because they can't work out the answer for themselves, then they are in need of advice. We aim not to give advice to anyone who is not a client, which means we charge to give advice.

Currently, quite a few people have got so used to finding information freely on the web that it has spilled over into their expectations generally. For example, they call us up wanting and expecting answers to their questions for free. This surprises me because nobody expects to get given a free meal in a restaurant or to go into a shop and walk away with clothes for free. However, advice is clearly not perceived as having a cost to give, so perhaps it is not valued. This probably stems from the view that the value of a lawyer is to do something concrete like draft a contract or register a trade mark. Yet advice is in my view the most valuable way I, as a lawyer, can help clients.

Even if businesses were on a very strict budget, and wanted to do their own legal work, they would be better off doing so by consulting an IP lawyer for strategic guidance to assess what to register, and what to prioritise.

Technological impact

While it is true that when it comes to legal advice from search engines, much of the content is generic, sometimes outdated, inaccurate or conflicting, it is conceivable that in a few years from now some online tools will provide a substitute for certain types of insight that are currently only obtainable through one-to-one advice.

In the meantime, when it comes to IP and compliance for online businesses, the law involved can sometimes be complex, and fast-changing, and can vary significantly depending on where you are based and the nature of your activities. Relying on web-based legal advice to decide what IP to register or which contract templates to buy isn't always possible or sensible.

However, given the development of artificial intelligence, with IBM's Watson beating contestants on a quiz show, it is possible that much of the advice not yet available through an online search will be available within the next five years. Consulting an experienced expert whose advice takes into account your particular circumstances may then no longer be necessary for many of the issues on which you might now consult a lawyer.

Law firms need to constantly upskill and ensure that value is added in ways which will enable them to remain relevant to the client. So, it is invaluable to get some feedback and insights from those clients.

The web is likely to result in many changes to the way the legal industry conducts its business in the years to come.

Difficulty of getting online success

The bottom line for success is to provide lots of freely available good content so that you will be discovered. To be found by potential customers looking for goods and services you provide, a rule of thumb could involve giving away as much as 80% of the value you have to offer, in order to encourage 20% of users to buy additional information or services from you.

This 'freemium' model of web business is a huge ongoing challenge to every industry, especially the law because it traditionally sells information.

Many businesses are struggling to give away so much information for free, and are worried that competitors will copy their content.

Conclusion

Traditionally, law was bounded by geography, culture, language, and more. Now we have a complex mix of global and local. There is pressure on law firms to do more-for-less. There are new providers taking elements of legal work, such as document review providers. And the legal profession is experiencing deep changes in the way people see lawyers.

The digital revolution has completely altered the relevance of IP law because everything digital is intangible, and IP law is the body of law that deals with intangibles.

About the author

 Shireen Smith qualified as a solicitor over 25 years ago and has extensive practical experience of intellectual property and technology law as well as a Masters in Intellectual Property Law from QMW, London University.

Having developed a good grasp of the IP issues relevant to blue chip companies as an in-house lawyer at Reuters, she then applied that knowledge to working with start-ups and SMEs once she founded Azrights in 2005.

Given Shireen's background working with software developers and trading room systems, it was inevitable that Azrights would focus on IT, technology and commercial issues as well as IP. She believes technology is of overriding relevance in today's digital economy, and aims to provide the A to Z of IP/IT services.

Shireen is the author of a successful book, *Legally Branded*, published in 2012. She blogs regularly and is frequently invited to speak on aspects of IP and entrepreneurship.

During her years in practice she has been exposed to a wide range of contentious and non-contentious IP, IT and internet law matters and, as a consequence, she is a 'lawyer for the digital world' who understands the practical aspects of branding, software, online marketing and media.

Shireen is passionate about entrepreneurship, the digital world and the internet revolution which are transforming business today.

She is also a member of many legal bodies, including the Society for Computers and Law, the International Division of the Law Society, and the International Trade mark Association, where she has sat on the Internet Committee. She has also had her work published by the Society for Computers and Law, Caritas, and Bloomsbuy's *QFinance*.

You can find her at

http://azrights.com
https://www.facebook.com/Azrights
http://www.shireensmith.com/blog
twitter.com/shireensmith
https://uk.linkedin.com/in/shireensmith

Lightning Source UK Ltd.
Milton Keynes UK
UKOW04f0148060816

280084UK00006B/38/P